D1440965

A Prayer Book

of

Catholic Devotions

A Prayer Book

of

Catholic Devotions

BX
2170
C55
S76
2004

*Praying the Seasons and Feasts
of the Church Year*

William G. Storey

LOYOLAPRESS.

CHICAGO

BX
2170
.C55S77
2004

LOYOLAPRESS.

3441 N. ASHLAND AVENUE
CHICAGO, ILLINOIS 60657
(800) 621-1008
WWW.LOYOLABOOKS.ORG

© 2004 William G. Storey
All rights reserved

Nihil Obstat	*Imprimatur*
Reverend Robert L. Tuzik, Ph.D.	Most Reverend Edwin M. Conway, D.D.
Censor Deputatus	Vicar General
September 8, 2003	Archdiocese of Chicago
	September 10, 2003

The *Nihil Obstat* and *Imprimatur* are official declarations that a book is free of doctrinal and moral error. No implicataion is contained therein that those who have granted the *Nihil Obstat* and *Imprimatur* agree with the content, opinions, or statements expressed. Nor do they assume any legal responsibility associated with publication.

Selected psalms and psalm verses are from *The Psalms: Grail Translation from the Hebrew* © 1993 by the Ladies of the Grail (England). Used by permission of GIA Publications, Inc., exclusive agent. All rights reserved.

Unless otherwise noted, the Scripture quotations contained herein are from the *New Revised Standard Version of the Bible* © 1989 Division of Christian Education of the National Council of Churches of Christ in the U.S.A. and are used by permission. All rights reserved.

Scripture passages cited as "TEV" are taken from *Today's English Version of the Bible: Good News Bible* (New York: American Bible Society, 1976, 1979).

The English translation of the Te Deum Laudamus, the Benedictus, and the Magnificat prepared by the English Language Liturgical Consultation (ELLC), 1988.

The English translations of the Litanies of the Sacred Heart of Jesus, the Precious Blood, and Loreto, and of the Ancient Prayer to the Virgin and the Salve, Regina, are from A Book of Prayers 1982, International Committee on English in the Liturgy, Inc. (ICEL); the English translation of the Opening Prayers from the Roman Missal is copyright 1973 by ICEL. All rights reserved.

Many of the prayers have been composed or translated from original sources by the author/compiler.

Acknowledgments continued on p. 275.

Cover design by Megan Duffy Rostan
Interior design by Donna Antkowiak

Library of Congress Cataloging-in-Publication Data
Storey, William George, 1923–
   A prayer book of Catholic devotions : praying the seasons
and feasts of the church year / William G. Storey.
      p. cm.
Includes bibliographical references.
   ISBN 0-8294-2030-4
   1. Church year—Prayer-books and devotions—English.
2. Catholic Church—Prayer-books and devotions—English.   I. Title.
   BX2170.C55S79 2003
   242'.802—dc22
                                                        2003017854

Printed in Hong Kong/China
04 05 06 07 08 RRD/G 10 9 8 7 6 5 4 3 2 1

Contents

The Church's Year of Grace   1

The Cycles of the Church Calendar 3
Forms of Popular Piety 4
The Home Altar 6
How to Use This Prayer Book 7
Group Prayer 8

The Season of Advent   11

The Advent Wreath 12
Advent Mealtime Prayers 13
A Daily Devotion for Advent 15
The Virgin Mary and Advent 22
A Novena in Honor of Our Lady of Guadalupe . . 23

The Season of Christmas   29

A Pre-Christmas Novena 29
Christmas Eve Customs 34
     The Proclamation of the Nativity 34
     The Blessing of the Crib 35
     The Blessing of the Tree 37
Christmas Meal Prayers 39
A Christmas Devotion 41
December 31, Vigil of New Year's Day 48
January 1, Solemnity of the Mother of God
    and the Octave of Christmas 53
Epiphany, the Baptism of the Lord, and
    the Presentation 58

The Season of Lent   69

Lenten Meal Prayers 70
Daily Devotions during Lent 71
A Devotion to the Five Wounds of
    Jesus Crucified 79
Another Devotion in Honor of
    the Five Wounds 84
A Devotion to the Precious Blood of Christ 88
A Devotion to the Sacred Heart of Jesus 93
The Fifteen O's 93
The Hours of the Passion 102
    Friday at Midmorning 103
    Friday at Noon 105
    Friday at Midafternoon 108
A Devotion in Honor of the Mother of Sorrows . . 110
Devotions for Holy Week 115
    Meal Prayers for Holy Week 115
    A Devotion to the Blessed Passion 116
Devotions for the Easter Triduum 124
    Holy Thursday Devotions 131
    Good Friday Devotions 132
    Holy Saturday Devotions 134

The Fifty Days of Easter   137

Meal Prayers for Eastertide 137
The *Regina Coeli* 140
Daily Devotions during Eastertide 140
    For Use on the Sundays of Eastertide . . . 140
    For Use on the Mondays, Wednesdays,
    and Fridays of Eastertide 147

For Use on the Tuesdays and Thursdays
of Eastertide **154**
The *Via Lucis* **162**
A Novena for Pentecost **184**

Post-Pentecostal Solemnities   193

A Devotion in Honor of the Holy Trinity **193**
A Devotion to the Blessed Sacrament
for Corpus Christi **200**
A Devotion to the Sacred Heart of Jesus **206**

Litanies and Insistent Prayer   213

Litany of the Sacred Heart of Jesus **214**
Litany of the Precious Blood of Jesus **217**
Litany of the Blessed Sacrament of the Altar . . . **219**
Litany of Our Lady (Loreto) **221**
Litany of the Blessed Virgin Mary **223**

The Rosary of the Blessed
Virgin Mary   227

Ways of Praying the Rosary **229**
The Joyful Mysteries **231**
The Luminous Mysteries **236**
The Sorrowful Mysteries **241**
The Glorious Mysteries **246**

A Biblical Way of the Cross   251

Notes **270**
Acknowledgments (cont.) **275**
About the Editor **278**

The Church's Year of Grace

Even before the invention of printing in the fifteenth century, popular books of prayer were best sellers. They multiplied among Catholics to assist them in their daily prayers and to accompany them on their annual pilgrimage through the liturgical year.

This is a *Catholic* prayer book because it contains those prayers and devotions which express the very heart and soul of Catholic Christianity. The central teachings of Jesus are presented by the Church in many ways, but never more fully than in its liturgy and popular devotions. The way the Church prays is the way it believes. Those who want to be genuine Catholics in both head and heart need to activate in prayer each day the central themes of our religion.

It is a *Catholic* prayer book in another sense, too. It presents devotions from all ages and by all kinds of Catholic believers. It is *universal* in two ways: It both contains some of the best of our long past and represents a universality of teaching and authentic religious feeling that binds us to all our fellow believers.

Catholic also means "orthodox": "correct praise." A Catholic prayer book shows us how to pray well, correctly, in tune with the tradition, without deviating from the norms of belief and holiness. It is a safe, reliable way of praying that leads us deeper and deeper into the fullness of the Church's liturgy, and it is never the expression of purely individual attitudes and feelings.

This is not an official prayer book like a Sacramentary, Lectionary, or Book of Hours. Nevertheless, it combines both official and unofficial forms of prayer that have found a place in the lives of past and present Catholics. It is a book of what are called *popular* devotions that are compatible with and supplement the official liturgy, thus encouraging a deeper participation in the liturgical year.

Liturgy is continuously overflowing into devotions, and devotions are often adopted as parts of the Liturgy. The Liturgy and the spirit of prayer are too rich and lively to be confined to the official books. Sometimes a liturgical text is actually an expression of a once-popular devotion that matured to the point of entering the official Liturgy. The feasts of the Holy Trinity, of the Blessed Sacrament (Corpus Christi), of the Sacred Heart of Jesus, and of the Rosary are good examples of popular devotions that entered the Liturgy as special feasts. As in every other aspect of its life, the Church grows both from the bottom and from the top. It never stops trying to appropriate and enjoy more fully what has been handed on from generation to generation. It never stops developing fresh forms of prayer that express and articulate the Good News.

When we use a term such as *popular,* as in "popular piety" or "popular devotions," we mean forms of prayer that belong to the people of God as a whole, and especially to the laity. A popular devotion or a popular prayer book is accessible to ordinary people; it is not too rich, too long, or too out of the ordinary for regular people to enjoy. It is vital to the daily and seasonal prayer of a wide cross section of Catholic Christians.

Alongside the Liturgy itself there is a treasured inheritance, a potent prayer force of popular devotions, that is indispensable to the Christian life. Pride in our spiritual heritage—the gift of martyrs, mystics, and saints of old and of the recent past—will inspire us to be faithful and consistent users of this treasury of holiness. Regular use of these devotions will bring its own solid, personal conviction about the value of such prayer and its connection to the Liturgy. Experience, conviction, and a deeper interior life will, in time and with the blessing of God, produce fresh forms of prayer and liturgy suitable to the third millennium.

> "What is new in the life of the Church emerges only from the Tradition."
> St. Stephen, bishop of Rome (254–257)

The Cycles of the Church Calendar

What we call *Ordinary Time* (about thirty-four weeks of the liturgical year) still reflects the decisions of the earliest period of Church history. The apostles or their immediate successors decided to keep the Jewish week of seven days but to set aside the old Sabbath and replace it with the Lord's day (Sunday). In the second century it was decided to highlight Friday, the day of Jesus' passion and death. And so the week is the fundamental unit of the Church's celebration of the mystery of Christ.

In addition to Ordinary Time, the Church gradually worked out a *Paschal Cycle* of weeks, the forty days of Lent and the fifty days of Easter. Lent was primarily a period of final preparation for those who were to be baptized during the Easter Vigil. Easter became a fifty-day celebration of new life in Christ through conversion and the sacraments of Baptism, Confirmation, and Eucharist. With the renewed interest in adult conversion and baptism since the Second Vatican Council, the Lent-Easter cycle has taken on fresh meaning for those preparing to be baptized and for those already baptized.

A little later the Church created the Cycle of the Incarnation. This cycle includes the season of Advent, culminating in the great festivals of Christmas, Epiphany, the Baptism of Jesus, and his Presentation in the Temple (February 2).

These two cycles focus our minds in a special way on the coming of Jesus into the world and on his exodus from the world as he returned to the Father after his saving work had been accomplished. With minds and hearts renewed each year by these celebrations, we prepare for his coming again in glory to judge the living and the dead. "Come, Lord Jesus!" (Revelation 22:20).

Forms of Popular Piety

The Sacred Liturgy itself is the chief and indispensable way of celebrating the divine mysteries of our religion and must take precedence over all kinds of private devotion. Forms of popular piety, however, assist us to understand and appreciate the Liturgy and to deepen our personal prayer life so that we come to the Liturgy with a heightened awareness of its beauty, content, and spiritual power to transform us in the likeness of Christ. As the Congregation for Divine Worship and the Discipline of the Sacraments has noted: "The history of the Western Church is marked by the flowering among the Christian people of multiple and varied expressions of simple and fervent faith in God, of love for Christ the Redeemer, of invocations of the Holy Spirit, of devotions to the Blessed Virgin Mary, of the veneration of the saints, of commitment to conversion and to fraternal charity."[1]

In English these forms of popular piety or popular religiosity are usually called devotions. The Congregation continues:

> Although not part of the Liturgy they are considered to be in harmony with the spirit, the norms, and rhythms of the Liturgy. Such pious exercises are inspired to some degree by the Liturgy and lead the Christian people to the Liturgy. . . . Many of these exercises are part of the cultic patrimony of particular churches or religious families. . . . Popular piety has rightly been regarded as "treasure of the people of God" and manifests a thirst for God known only to the poor and the humble, rendering them capable of a generosity and of sacrifice to the point of heroism in testifying to the faith while displaying an acute sense of the profound attributes of God. . . . It also generates interior attitudes otherwise rarely seen to the same degree: patience, an awareness of the Cross in everyday life, detachment, openness to others and devotion. . . .
>
> Popular piety is also characterized by a great variety and richness of bodily gestures and symbolic expressions: kissing or touching of images, relics and sacred objects; pilgrimages, processions, . . . kneeling and prostrating; wearing of medals and badges. These are direct and simple ways of giving external expression to the heart and to one's commitment to live the Christian life.[2]

The devotions presented here use psalms, canticles and readings from the Bible, traditional prayers from many sources, and the pious patterns of prayer from many different centuries and backgrounds. This approach is in keeping with the instruction of the Church: "While drawn up in terms less exacting than those employed for the prayers of the Liturgy, devotional prayers and formulae should be inspired by Sacred Scripture, the Liturgy, the Fathers of the Church and the Magisterium, and concord with the Church's faith."[3]

The Home Altar

Another characteristic of popular devotion is the *home altar.* Long before Christians built churches for public prayer, they worshipped daily in their homes. In order to orient their prayer (to *orient* means literally "to turn toward the east"), they painted or hung a cross on the east wall of their main room. This practice was in keeping with ancient Jewish tradition ("Look toward the east, O Jerusalem," Baruch 4:36); Christians turned in that direction when they prayed morning and evening and at other times. This expression of their undying belief in the coming again of Jesus was united to their conviction that the cross, "the sign of the Son of Man," would appear in the eastern heavens on his return (see Matthew 24:30).

Building on that ancient custom, devout Catholics often have a home altar, shrine, or prayer corner containing a crucifix, religious pictures (icons), Bible, holy water, lights, and flowers as part of the essential furniture of a Christian home. Often erected on a shelf or table in the living or dining room, the family assembles there before or after meals at day's beginning and at day's ending. Many Catholics keep a perpetual candle burning on the home altar to remind themselves of Christ's promise: "Where two or three are gathered in my name, I am there among them" (Matthew 18:20).[4]

How to Use This Prayer Book

Many people who use this prayer book will probably pray it in private and by themselves. Others, however, will find it useful for family prayer or with a group of friends, in prayer groups, or at church meetings.

Before beginning any of these devotions, the first thing to remember is that God is present everywhere and hears every word we utter, silently or vocally. The second great fact is that by holy Baptism we are the shrines of the Holy Spirit, who calls out without ceasing: "Abba, Father!" (see Mark 14:36; Romans 8:15; Galatians 4:6).

Mindful of these central theological principles, we pause for a few moments of silence before starting our prayer. The pauses that are suggested elsewhere in the text are equally helpful. In private recitation we may stop briefly whenever we feel called to dwell on phrases that particularly move our minds and hearts.

The hymns, psalms, canticles, readings, and other prayers are traditional and precious resources for our very personal prayer. They come from the rich and many-layered treasure of Catholic piety that has inspired and assisted generations of Christians in learning how to pray well.

Each sacred text should be recited with the attention and devotion it deserves. We are addressing the Maker of the Universe and cannot afford to be casual about it! The prophets, priests, and saints who put these texts at our disposal urge us to pray both with the lips and with the heart.

People who pray alone may sit, stand, or kneel as they see fit, but they must remember that they do so in the presence of the whole court of heaven.

People who pray in families or other groups may adopt some set of postures that facilitate common prayer: standing for hymns, psalms, and canticles; sitting for readings and meditation; kneeling for intercessions and the final prayers. Change of posture is often helpful to recollection and attention.

Gestures—the sign of the cross, bowing at references to the Holy Trinity, hands extended during the Lord's Prayer, a kiss of peace at the end of the devotions, and others—are very helpful to both common and private prayer.

Group Prayer

Prayer in families or other small groups is facilitated by having both a *Leader* of prayer and a *Reader* for the Scripture lessons when they are present.

The *Leader* should
❖ call the group to silent prayer and initiate the vocal prayer
❖ alternate the stanzas of the hymns, psalms, and canticles with the group
❖ call for silent or spontaneous prayer where it is indicated after psalms, readings, or at the close of the intercessions
❖ begin the first few words of the antiphon (refrain) before a psalm or canticle and lead its repetition at its close or even between every stanza

- ❖ lead the petitions of a litany or of intercessions
- ❖ pray the closing prayers
- ❖ encourage the group to respond to the prayers and to voice their petitions during the pause for intercessory prayer

The *Reader* reads the Scripture lessons aloud.

A note on the name of God: In what are called the "Grail Psalms"[5] and some of the biblical canticles used in this book, the unutterable name of God in Hebrew (its letters in English are *YHWH*) is represented by the word LORD. The name derives from the verb *to be* and indicates the God who was and is and will be present to the human race, and in a particular way to the people of the covenant.

A note on symbols: Throughout the text the cross [✝] indicates that those praying should make the sign of the cross. The tilde [~] followed by text in small capital letters indicates a response by a group or a person other than the leader of prayer. For example: ~AMEN; ~HOSANNA IN THE HIGHEST!

These forms of prayer might be unfamiliar to some people, but a bit of patience and attention will show how helpful they are to devotional growth. They both supplement and complement the Sacred Liturgy and make us appreciate the power and insight of popular devotions.

How to Pray

When you stand up for prayer,
do not begin in a slovenly way,
lest you perform all your prayer
in a slack or slovenly or wearied way.
Rather, when you stand up,
sign your self with the sign of the cross,
gather together your thoughts,
be in a state of recollection and readiness,
gaze upon him to whom you are praying,
and then commence.[6]

Evagrius of Pontus (c. 345–399)

The Season of Advent

Popular piety is awestruck at the prospect of God taking flesh in the womb of the humble and lowly Virgin Mary. The faithful are particularly sensitive to the difficulties faced by the Virgin Mary during her pregnancy, and are deeply moved by the fact that there was not room at the inn for Joseph and Mary, just as she was about to give birth to the Christ Child (Luke 2:7).[7]

Advent is a time of waiting, of conversion, and of hope.

❖ *waiting:* memory of the first, humble coming of the Lord in our mortal flesh;

❖ *waiting:* supplication for his final, glorious coming as Lord of history and universal judge;

❖ *conversion:* to which the liturgy at this time often refers, quoting the prophets, especially John the Baptist: "Repent, for the kingdom of heaven is at hand!" (Matthew 3:2 NKJV).

❖ joyful *hope* that the salvation already accomplished by Christ (see Romans 8:24–25) and the reality of grace in the world will mature and reach their fullness, thereby granting us what is promised by faith, and "we will be like him, for we will see him as he is" (1John 3:2).

The Advent Wreath

In Canada and the United States, the Advent wreath has become a prominent item in both home and church. Four candles, three purple and one pink, are set in an evergreen wreath and lighted progressively each evening as the four weeks of Advent unfold. The wreath is usually set in the middle of the dining-room table or on the family altar, and the prayers of each Sunday of Advent are recited as each candle is lighted before dinner each day.

First Week

All-powerful God,
increase our strength of will for doing good
that Christ may find an eager welcome at his
    coming
and call us to his side in the kingdom of heaven,
where he lives and reigns with you and the Holy
    Spirit
one God, forever and ever.
~AMEN.[8]

Second Week

God of power and mercy,
open our hearts in welcome.
Remove the things that hinder us
from receiving Christ with joy
so that we may share his wisdom
and become one with him
when he comes in glory,
for he lives and reigns with you and the Holy
    Spirit,

one God, forever and ever.
~AMEN.[9]

Third Week
Lord God,
may we, your people,
who look forward to the birthday of Christ
experience the joy of salvation
and celebrate that feast with love and
   thanksgiving.
We ask this through Christ our Lord.
~AMEN.[10]

Fourth Week
Father, all-powerful God,
your eternal Word took flesh on our earth
when the Virgin Mary placed her life
at the service of your plan.
Lift our minds in watchful hope
to hear the voice which announces his glory
and open our minds to receive the Spirit
who prepares us for his coming.
We ask this through Christ our Lord.
~AMEN.[11]

Advent Mealtime Prayers
Before Dinner
LEADER: Blessed is the One † who comes in the
   name of the Lord.

ALL: ~HOSANNA IN THE HIGHEST!

PRAYER

All-powerful God,
increase our will for doing good
that Christ may find an eager welcome when
   he comes
to call us to his side in the kingdom of heaven,
where he lives and reigns with you and the Holy
   Spirit,
one God, forever and ever.
ALL: ~AMEN.

LEADER: Lord, have mercy.
ALL: ~CHRIST, HAVE MERCY. LORD, HAVE MERCY.

LEADER: Our Father . . . *(Continue in unison.)*
LEADER: Bless † us, O Lord, and these your gifts
which we are about to receive from your bounty;
through Christ our Lord.
ALL: ~AMEN.

LEADER: May the King of eternal glory
make us sit at his welcome table in heaven.
ALL: ~AMEN.

After Dinner

LEADER: Drop down dew, you heavens from
   above,
ALL: ~AND LET THE EARTH BUD FORTH A SAVIOR.

LEADER: See, I come quickly, says the Lord.
ALL: ~AMEN. COME, LORD JESUS!

LEADER: Glory to the Father, and to the Son,
and to the Holy Spirit:
ALL: ~AS IT WAS IN THE BEGINNING, IS NOW,
AND WILL BE FOREVER. AMEN.

LEADER: God of love and truth,
you loved the world so much
that you sent your only Son to be our Savior
and from a Virgin brought him forth
for the world to see.
May we receive him as our Lord and Brother
and celebrate him as our gracious Redeemer.
We ask this through the same Christ our Lord.
ALL: ~AMEN.

LEADER: Almighty God,
we give you thanks for these and for all your gifts.
You live and reign forever and ever.
ALL: ~AMEN.

LEADER: Reward with eternal life, O Lord,
all those who do us good for your name's sake.
ALL: ~AMEN.

LEADER: May the souls of the faithful departed
through the mercy of God rest in peace.
ALL: ~AMEN.

A Daily Devotion for Advent

In the northern hemisphere the winter solstice is celebrated by many people because of the happy coincidence of the celebration of the birth of Jesus with the significant change of the seasons marked by the winter solstice. Christmas itself on December 25 is aligned with both March 25, the feast of his conception, and with the birth of John the Baptist on June 24, the old summer solstice. Just as the light of the sun begins once more to grow stronger at the winter solstice, so in our Advent prayers we greet the new light of Christ at his birth and ask for that light to increase in our lives.

Your light will come, O Jerusalem.
~THE LORD WILL DAWN ON YOU IN RADIANT BEAUTY.

We shall see the glory of the Lord,
~THE SPLENDOR OF OUR GOD.

The sign of the cross shall appear in the heavens,
~WHEN OUR LORD SHALL COME TO JUDGE THE WORLD.

AN ADVENT HYMN

Comfort my people and quiet her fear;
Tell her the time of salvation draws near.
Tell her I come to remove all her shame;
"She that is pitied" shall be her new name.

Say to the cities of Judah: "Behold!
Gentle, yet mighty, the arm of the Lord
Rescues the captives of darkness and sin,
Bringing them justice and joy without end."

Mountains and hills shall become like a plain.
Vanished are mourning and hunger and pain;
Never again shall these war against you;
"See, he comes quickly to make all things new."
Amen.[12]

Psalm 145:1–13   Praise God's Glory

Antiphon You are the bright and the morning
    star, O Christ our Lord.

I will give you glory, O God, my king,
I will bless your name forever.

I will bless you day after day
and praise your name forever.
You are great, Lord, highly to be praised,
your greatness cannot be measured.

Age to age shall proclaim your works,
shall declare your mighty deeds,
shall speak of your splendor and glory,
tell the tale of your wonderful works.

They will speak of your terrible deeds,
recount your greatness and might.
They will recall your abundant goodness;
age to age shall ring out your justice.

You are kind and full of compassion,
slow to anger, abounding in love.
How good you are, Lord, to all,
compassionate to all your creatures.

All your creatures shall thank you, O Lord,
and your friends shall repeat their blessing.
They shall speak of the glory of your reign
and declare your might, O God,

to make known to all your mighty deeds
and the glorious splendor of your reign.
Yours is an everlasting kingdom;
your rule lasts from age to age.

ANTIPHON YOU ARE THE BRIGHT AND THE MORNING STAR, O CHRIST OUR LORD.

PSALM PRAYER

Let us pray *(pause for quiet prayer):*

God of kindness and compassion,
may we speak of your glorious reign
established by Jesus the Messiah
and thank you with full hearts
for his coming to live among us
as our teacher, our model, and our Savior.
Blest be the name of Jesus!
~AMEN.

THE LORD
OUR SALVATION

READING **ISAIAH 52:7–10**

How beautiful upon the mountains are the feet of the messenger who announces peace, who brings good news, who announces salvation, who says to Zion, "Your God reigns." Listen! Your sentinels lift up their voices, together they sing for joy; for in plain sight they see the return of the LORD to Zion. . . . The LORD has bared his holy arm before the eyes of all the nations; and all the ends of the earth shall see the salvation of our God.

SILENCE

RESPONSE

The Sun of righteousness will arise
~WITH HEALING IN HIS WINGS.

OR THIS READING   GOD'S HOUSE   ISAIAH 2:1–3

In days to come the mountain of the LORD's house shall be established as the highest of the mountains, and shall be raised above the hills; all the nations shall stream to it. Many peoples shall come and say, "Come, let us go up to the mountain of the LORD, to the house of the God of Jacob; that he may teach us his ways and that we may walk in his paths."

SILENCE

RESPONSE

Let your face shine on us, O Lord of hosts,
~AND WE SHALL BE SAVED.

CANTICLE OF ZACHARY   LUKE 1:68–79[13]

ANTIPHON   LIKE THE SUN IN THE MORNING,
THE SAVIOR OF THE WORLD WILL DAWN.
LIKE RAIN ON THE MEADOWS HE WILL DESCEND.

Blessed † are you, Lord, the God of Israel,
you have come to your people and set them free.
You have raised up for us a mighty Savior,
born of the house of your servant David.

Through your holy prophets, you promised of old
    to save us from our enemies,
    from the hands of all who hate us,
    to show mercy to our forebears,
    and to remember your holy covenant.

This was the oath you swore to our father
    Abraham:
        to set us free from the hands of our enemies,
        free to worship you without fear,
        holy and righteous before you,
        all the days of our life.

And you, my child, shall be called the prophet
    of the Most High,
for you will go before the Lord to prepare the way,
to give God's people knowledge of salvation
by the forgiveness of their sins.

In the tender compassion of our God
the dawn from on high shall break upon us,
to shine on those who dwell in darkness
    and the shadow of death,
and to guide our feet into the way of peace.

Glory to the Holy and Undivided Trinity:
now and always and forever and ever. Amen.

ANTIPHON LIKE THE SUN IN THE MORNING,
THE SAVIOR OF THE WORLD WILL DAWN.
LIKE RAIN ON THE MEADOWS HE WILL DESCEND.

INTERCESSIONS

Blessed be Jesus Christ, the joy of all who wait
    for his coming.
~COME, LORD JESUS.

Jesus, Son of the Most High, whose coming was
    announced

to the Virgin Mary by the angel Gabriel,
~COME, AND RULE YOUR CHOSEN PEOPLE.

Holy One of God, whom John recognized
while still in his mother's womb,
~COME, AND BRING JOY TO THE WORLD.

Jesus, whose precious name was revealed
to Joseph by an angel,
~COME, AND SAVE YOUR PEOPLE FROM THEIR SINS.

Lord Jesus, light of the Magi and all the gentiles,
~COME, AND REVEAL YOURSELF TO ALL THE NATIONS.

Light of the world, awaited and recognized
by old Simeon and Anna in the temple,
~COME, AND COMFORT YOUR PEOPLE.

(Pause for special intentions.)

THE LORD'S PRAYER

CLOSING PRAYER
God of love and mercy,
help us to follow the example of Mary,
always ready to do your will.
At the message of an angel
she welcomed your eternal Son
and, filled with the light of the Spirit,
she became the temple of your Word,
who lives and reigns with you and the Holy Spirit.
one God, forever and ever.
~AMEN.[14]

May the Lord Jesus, who is coming in glory
to judge the living and the dead,
✝ bless us and keep us.
~AMEN.

The Virgin Mary and Advent

The Liturgy frequently celebrates the Blessed Virgin
Mary in an exemplary way during the season of Advent.
It recalls the women of the Old Testament who prefig-
ured and prophesied her mission; it exalts her faith and
the humility with which she promptly and totally submit-
ted to God's plan of salvation; it highlights her presence
in the events of grace preceding the birth of the Savior.

The approach of Christmas is celebrated throughout
the American continent with many displays of popular
piety centered on the Feast of Our Lady of Guadalupe
(December 12), which dispose the faithful to receive the
Savior at his birth. Mary, "who was intimately united with
the birth of the Church in America, became the radiant
star illuminating the proclamation of Christ the Savior to
the members of these nations."[15]

THE ANNUNCIATION

Salvation to all who will is nigh,
That All, which always is All everywhere,
Which cannot sin and yet all sins must bear,
Which cannot die, yet cannot choose but die,
Lo, faithful Virgin, yields himself to lie
In prison, in thy womb; and though he there
Can take no sin, nor thou give, yet he will wear
Taken from thence, flesh, which death's force
    may try.

Ere by the spheres time was created, thou
Wast in his mind, who is thy son, and brother,
Whom thou conceiv'st, conceived; yea thou art now
Thy Maker's maker, and thy Father's mother;
Thou hast light in dark; and shutt'st in little room,
Immensity cloistered in thy dear womb.

John Donne (1572–1631)

A Novena in Honor of Our Lady of Guadalupe (December 3–11)

Mary appeared in the New World just ten years after the merciless conquest of Mexico. Her affectionate encounters in December 1531 with Saint Juan Diego, a poor, Christian campesino, and her promises of protection and compassion proclaimed her the Mother of the Americas, the consolation of the afflicted, and the special protector of the poor and oppressed. Her miraculous image is preserved and venerated in her basilica in Mexico City by millions of pilgrims each year. Her feast day falls on December 12, the last day of her three appearances to Juan Diego, and is celebrated throughout the Americas as an intimate part of Advent.

Mary conversed with Juan Diego and unveiled her precious will:

Know and be certain in your heart that I am the Ever-Virgin Holy Mary, Mother of the God of Great Truth, Teotl, of the One through Whom We Live, the Creator of Persons, the Owner of What Is Near and Together, of the Lord of Heaven and Earth. I very much want and ardently desire that my hermitage be erected is this place. In it I will show and give to all people all my love, my

The Season of Advent **23**

compassion, my help, and my protection,
because I am your merciful mother and the
mother of all the nations that live on this earth
who would love me, who would speak with me,
who would search for me, and who would place
their confidence in me. There I would hear their
laments and remedy and cure all their miseries,
misfortunes and sorrows.[16]

In the name of the Father, ✝ and of the Son,
and of the Holy Spirit.
~AMEN.

A MARIAN HYMN
Mother of Christ, our hope, our patroness,
Star of the sea, our beacon in distress,
Guide to the shores of everlasting day
God's holy people on their pilgrim way.

Virgin, in you God made his dwelling place;
Mother of all the living, full of grace,
Blessed are you: God's word you did believe;
"Yes" on your lips undid the "No" of Eve.

Daughter of God, who bore his holy One,
Dearest of all to Christ, your loving Son,
Show us his face, O Mother, as on earth,
Loving us all, you gave our Savior birth.[17]

A MARIAN ANTHEM   JUDITH 13:18–20; 15:9[18]
ANTIPHON ALL GENERATIONS WILL CALL ME BLESSED.

The Most High God has blessed you
more than any woman on earth.

How worthy of praise is the Lord God
who created heaven and earth!
He guided you as you cut off the head
of our deadliest enemy.

~ALL GENERATIONS WILL CALL ME BLESSED.

Your trust in God will never be forgotten
by those who tell of God's power.
May God give you everlasting honor
for what you have done.

~ALL GENERATIONS WILL CALL ME BLESSED.

May God reward you with blessings,
because you remained faithful to him
and did not hesitate to risk your own life
to relieve the oppression of your people.

~ALL GENERATIONS WILL CALL ME BLESSED.

You are Jerusalem's crowning glory,
the heroine of Israel,
the pride and joy of our people.

~ALL GENERATIONS WILL CALL ME BLESSED.

Glory to the Holy and Undivided Trinity.

~ALL GENERATIONS WILL CALL ME BLESSED.

Now and always and forever and ever. Amen.

~ALL GENERATIONS WILL CALL ME BLESSED.

PRAYER

Let us pray *(pause for quiet prayer):*

Great Mother of God, Mary most holy,

you risked everything in becoming
the Virgin Mother of the Messiah.
May we never forget your faith and trust
in the grace and power of God
and rely on your prayers,
now and forever.
~AMEN.

READING   MARY OF NAZARETH   LUKE 1:26–28, 31–32

The angel Gabriel was sent by God to a town in
Galilee called Nazareth, to a virgin engaged to a
man whose name was Joseph, of the house of
David. The virgin's name was Mary. And he came
to her and said, "Greetings, favored one! The Lord
is with you. . . . You will conceive in your womb
and bear a son, and you will name him Jesus. He
will be great, and will be called Son of the Most
High."

SILENCE

RESPONSE
Blessed are you among women, O Mary,
~AND BLESSED IS THE FRUIT OF YOUR WOMB, JESUS.

CANTICLE OF THE BLESSED VIRGIN MARY   LUKE 1:46–55[19]

ANTIPHON RADIANT MOTHER OF GOD,
COMFORTER OF THE AFFLICTED
AND CAUSE OF OUR JOY, COME TO OUR ASSISTANCE,
   ALLELUIA!

My soul ✝ proclaims the greatness of the Lord,
my spirit rejoices in God my Savior,
for you, Lord, have looked with favor on your
 lowly servant.

From this day all generations will call me blessed:
 you, the Almighty, have done great things
  for me
 and holy is your name.
 You have mercy on those who fear you,
  from generation to generation.

You have shown strength with your arm
and scattered the proud in their conceit,
casting down the mighty from their thrones
 and lifting up the lowly.
You have filled the hungry with good things
and sent the rich away empty.

You have come to the aid of your servant Israel,
to remember the promise of mercy,
the promise made to our forebears,
to Abraham and his children forever.

Glory to the Father, and to the Son,
and to the Holy Spirit:
as it was in the beginning, is now,
and will be forever. Amen.

ANTIPHON RADIANT MOTHER OF GOD,
COMFORTER OF THE AFFLICTED
AND CAUSE OF OUR JOY, COME TO OUR ASSISTANCE,
 ALLELUIA!

LITANY OF THE BLESSED VIRGIN MARY
(SEE PAGES 221–223 OR 223–225)

NOVENA PRAYER
We turn to you for protection,
holy Mother of God.
Listen to our prayers
and help us in our needs.
(Here we state our needs.)
Save us from every danger,
glorious and blessed Virgin.[20]

CLOSING PRAYER
God of power and mercy,
you blessed the Americas at Tepeyac
with the presence of the Virgin Mary of Guadalupe.
May her prayers help all men and women
to accept each other as brothers and sisters.
Through your justice present in our hearts
may social justice and peace reign in the world.
Please grant this through Christ our Lord.
~AMEN.[21]

May the Virgin Mary of Guadalupe
✝ be the joy and consolation of her people.
~AMEN.

The Season of Christmas

A Pre-Christmas Novena (December 16–24)

In many parts of the Catholic world, and especially in Mexico and the Southwest of the United States, people celebrate an annual novena during the nine days before Christmas known as *Las Posadas, jornada de Maria santisima y de San Jose de Nazaret a Belen* (The Shelters, a journey of Holy Mary and Saint Joseph from Nazareth to Bethlehem). In parishes people go from house to house in procession looking for a place for the holy family to rest, and celebrate these occasions with song, music, food, and sometimes short dramas. In the spirit of Las Posadas, the following devotion may serve as a preparation for the coming of the Christ child.

Christ is born for us, alleluia!

~COME, LET US ADORE HIM, ALLELUIA!

A MARIAN HYMN

O Queen of Heaven, to you the angels sing,
The Maiden-Mother of their Lord and King;
O Woman raised above the stars, receive
The homage of your children, sinless Eve.

O full of grace, in grace your womb did bear
Emmanuel, King David's promised heir;
O Eastern Gate, whom God had made his own,
By you God's glory came to Zion's throne.

O Burning Bush, you gave the world its light
When Christ your Son was born on Christmas
    night;
O Mary Queen, who bore God's holy One,
For us, your children, pray to God your Son.
Amen.[22]

READING   **MESSIANIC PROMISES**   **ISAIAH 61:1–2**
The spirit of the LORD God is upon me, because
the LORD has anointed me; he has sent me to
bring good news to the oppressed, to bind up the
brokenhearted, to proclaim liberty to the captives,
and release to the prisoners; to proclaim the year
of the LORD's favor.

SILENCE

RESPONSE
All the ends of the earth, alleluia!
~HAVE SEEN THE SALVATION OF OUR GOD, ALLELUIA!

THE O ANTIPHONS FOR MARY'S CANTICLE
*Pray the antiphon appropriate for the day before
and after the canticle below.*

December 16: O Wisdom, breath of the Most High, pervading and controlling all creation, mightily but tenderly ordering all things: ~COME, AND MAKE US FRIENDS OF GOD.

December 17: O Lord of lords and Leader of the house of Israel, who appeared to Moses in the burning bush and gave him the Law on Sinai: ~COME, AND SAVE US WITH YOUR MIGHTY ARM.

December 18: O Root of Jesse, standing as a signal to the nations, before whom all rulers shall keep silent and to whom the nations shall do homage: ~COME, AND SAVE US, DELAY NO LONGER.

December 19: O Key of David and Ruler of the house of Israel, when you open no one can close, and when you close no one can open: ~COME, PROCLAIM LIBERTY TO CAPTIVES AND SET PRISONERS FREE.

December 20: O radiant Dawn, Splendor of eternal light, and Sun of righteousness: ~COME, SHINE ON THOSE WHO WALK IN DARKNESS AND IN THE SHADOW OF DEATH.

December 21: O Ruler of the nations, the One they long for, the Cornerstone that binds all together: ~COME, AND SAVE THOSE YOU FASHIONED FROM THE DUST OF THE EARTH.

December 22: O Emmanuel, God-with-us, the Anointed of the nations and their Savior: ~COME, AND SET US FREE, O LORD OUR GOD.

December 23: O Savior of the world, you have risen like the sun in the morning sky and have descended into the womb of the Virgin like fine dew on the grass: ~Come, visit your people and redeem them.

December 24: O holy Mother of God, you are more worthy of honor than the cherubim and far more glorious than the seraphim: ~Come, and present your Son to the nations.

The Canticle of the Virgin Mary   Luke 1:46–55[23]

Antiphon (*The proper antiphon is read.*)

My soul † proclaims the greatness of the Lord,
my spirit rejoices in God my Savior,
for you, Lord, have looked with favor
on your lowly servant.

From this day all generations will call me blessed:
    you, the Almighty, have done great things
      for me
    and holy is your name.
    You have mercy on those who fear you,
    from generation to generation.

You have shown strength with your arm
and scattered the proud in their conceit,
casting down the mighty from their thrones
    and lifting up the lowly.
You have filled the hungry with good things
and sent the rich away empty.

You have come to the aid of your servant Israel,
to remember the promise of mercy,
the promise made to our forebears,
to Abraham and his children forever.

Glory to the Father, and to the Son,
and to the Holy Spirit:
as it was in the beginning, is now,
and will be forever. Amen.

(The proper antiphon is repeated.)

LITANY OF THE BLESSED VIRGIN MARY
(SEE PAGES 221–223 OR 223–225)

NOVENA PRAYER
Gracious God,
by the loving prayers of Mary and Joseph,
make us ready to welcome the Christ Child
who comes to proclaim the reign of God
and sets us free from sin and error.
Please hear the needs we present before you
as we praise, thank, and adore you
for the radiant presence of your beloved Son,
who lives and reigns with you and the Holy Spirit,
now and forever.
~AMEN.

May the Word made flesh, who came to live
    among us,
✝ bless us and keep us.
~AMEN.

Christmas Eve Customs

A variety of Catholic customs are observed on Christmas Eve before Midnight Mass: a special Christmas meal, carol singing, the blessing of the crib and the Christmas tree, and attendance at a vigil of hymns, readings, and prayers that is popular in many parish churches before the Midnight Mass.

The Proclamation of the Nativity [24]

Many ages after the creation of the world,
when in the beginning God made the heavens
   and the earth,
long after the Flood and the primeval covenant
   made with Noah,
more than two thousand years after the promises
   made to our father Abraham
   and our mother Sarah,
fifteen centuries after Moses and Miriam
   and the exodus from Egypt,
one thousand years after David was anointed king
   of Israel,
in the sixty-fifth week according to the prophecy
   of Daniel,
in the one hundred and ninety-fourth Olympiad,
in the year seven hundred and fifty-two
   from the founding of the city of Rome,
in the forty-second year of the emperor Augustus
   Caesar,
and in the sixth age of the world,
   while the whole earth lay in peace,

in order to consecrate the world by his gracious
   coming,
   JESUS THE CHRIST,
eternal God and Son of the everlasting Father,
conceived in time by the overshadowing of the
   Holy Spirit,
nine months having elapsed since his conception,
was born of the Virgin Mary in Bethlehem of
   Judea,
   GOD MADE MAN.
This is the birthday according to the flesh
   of our Lord Jesus Christ.

The Blessing of the Crib

The crib (or manger) is best placed on the family altar
or a low table. After the Christmas Eve dinner, families
may have the children sing a popular carol, read a les-
son from Luke's Gospel, place the figures in the crib,
and conclude with the collect prayer of Christmas. The
crib and the tree may be sprinkled with holy water during the blessings. According to our Catholic traditions it
is best to erect both the crib and the tree in the last
days of Advent and maintain them until the end of the
Christmas season.

In the name of the Father, ✝ and of the Son,
and of the Holy Spirit.
~AMEN.

(Sing a Christmas carol.)

A READING FROM THE HOLY GOSPEL ACCORDING TO ST. LUKE 2:1–20

In those days a decree went out from Emperor Augustus . . . as it had been told them. This is the Gospel of the Lord.

ALL: ~PRAISE TO YOU, LORD JESUS CHRIST.

PRAYER OF BLESSING

Jesus of Bethlehem,
you came down from heaven
to teach us that we are all the children of God,
beloved of the Father, and temples of the Holy
    Spirit.
Bless ✝ this crib of ours,
as we meditate on your loving care for us
that calls us to love you with all our hearts
and our neighbor as ourselves.
Jesus of the crib and of the cross,
be with us, now and forever.
~AMEN.

PRAYER

Almighty and merciful God,
by the birth of your only-begotten Son
in the stable of Bethlehem,
set us free from the bondage of sin
and bring us into the land of peace and plenty,
through the same Christ our Lord.
~AMEN.

The Blessing of the Tree

The Christmas tree represents the Tree of Paradise from which we stem and towards which we tend. Its ornaments remind us of the precious fruit of our redemption available to everyone for the asking. The tree is kept up at least from Christmas Eve through the Feast of Epiphany and the Feast of the Baptism of the Lord. Like the Advent wreath and the crib, it is a sacramental that reminds us of the great truths of the Christmas season.

PSALM 96:1–3, 10–13

ANTIPHON LET ALL THE TREES OF THE WOOD SHOUT FOR JOY!

O sing a new song to the LORD,
sing to the LORD all the earth.
O sing to the LORD, bless his name.

Proclaim God's help day by day,
tell among the nations his glory
and his wonders among all the peoples.

Proclaim to the nations: "God is king."
The world was made firm in its place;
God will judge the people in fairness.

Let the heavens rejoice and earth be glad,
let the sea and all within it thunder praise,
let the land and all it bears rejoice,
all the trees of the wood shout for joy

at the presence of the LORD who comes,
who comes to rule the earth,
comes with justice to rule the world,
and to judge the peoples with truth.

Glory to the Father, and to the Son,
and to the Holy Spirit:
as it was in the beginning, is now,
and will be forever. Amen.

ANTIPHON LET ALL THE TREES OF THE WOOD SHOUT
FOR JOY!

PSALM PRAYER

Let us pray *(pause for quiet prayer):*

O God, great and worthy of all praise,
creation bows down before you
in honor of the coming of our blessed Savior.
By the prayers of his holy mother Mary,
assist us in worshipping the Christ Child
who gladdens the whole world.
We ask this through the same Christ our Lord.
~AMEN.

A READING FROM THE PROPHET ISAIAH 9:6–7

A child has been born for us, a son given to us;
authority rests upon his shoulders;
and he is named Wonderful Counselor,
Mighty God, Everlasting Father, Prince of Peace.
His authority shall grow continually,
and there shall be endless peace for the throne of
    David and his kingdom.
He will establish and uphold it with justice and
    with righteousness
from this time onward and forevermore.

RESPONSE

The Word was made flesh, alleluia!

~AND CAME TO LIVE AMONG US, ALLELUIA!

Christmas Eve Prayer

God our Father,
every year we rejoice
as we look forward to this feast of our salvation.
May we welcome Christ as our Redeemer,
and meet him with confidence
when he comes to be our judge.
He lives and reigns with you and the Holy Spirit,
one God, now and forever.
~AMEN.

Christmas Meal Prayers
(December 24–February 2)

Before Dinner

LEADER: The Word was made flesh, alleluia!

ALL: ~AND CAME TO LIVE AMONG US, ALLELUIA!

LEADER: Father of our Lord Jesus Christ,
our glory is to stand before the world
    as your sons and daughters.
May the simple beauty of Jesus' birth
summon us to love what is most deeply human,
and to see your Word made flesh
reflected in those whose lives we touch.
We ask this through Christ our Lord.

ALL: ~Amen.[25]

LEADER: Lord, have mercy.
ALL: ~Christ, have mercy. Lord, have mercy.

LEADER: Our Father . . . *(Continue in unison.)*

LEADER: Bless ✝ us, O Lord, and these your gifts
which we are about to receive from your
bounty;
through Christ our Lord.
ALL: ~Amen.

LEADER: May the King of eternal glory
make us sit at his welcome table.
ALL: ~Amen.

After Dinner

LEADER: Glory to God in the highest, alleluia!
ALL: ~And peace to God's people on earth,
alleluia!

LEADER: May your name be praised,
Lord our God,
from the rising to the setting of the sun,
and through the prayers of Mary and Joseph
unite our families in peace and love.
We ask this in the name of Jesus.
ALL: ~Amen.

LEADER: Almighty God,
we give you thanks for food and drink

and all your gifts to us.
You live and reign forever and ever.

ALL: ~AMEN.

LEADER: Reward with eternal life, O Lord,
all those who do us good
for your name's sake.

ALL: ~AMEN.

LEADER: May the souls of the faithful departed
through the mercy of God rest in peace.

ALL: ~AMEN.

A Christmas Devotion

It was probably St. Francis of Assisi (1181–1226) who first erected a Christmas scene; filled it with straw, an empty crib, an ox, and an ass; and had Mass celebrated there Christmas Eve. He himself sang the Gospel of the Midnight Mass and said the words tasted like honey and the honeycomb. Ever since then, the Franciscans have been famous for their devotion to the Christ Child and to the mysteries of the Christmas cycle of feasts. The following devotion is traditional in the Capuchin Franciscan Order and is recited before the Christmas crib in church or at home during the whole of Christmastide.

The Happy Morn

This is the month, and this the happy morn,
Wherein the Son of heaven's eternal King,
Of wedded Maid and Virgin Mother born,
Our great redemption from above did bring;

For so the holy sages once did sing,
    That he our deadly forfeit should release,
And with his Father work us a perpetual peace.

That glorious form, that light unsufferable,
And that far-beaming blaze of majesty,
Wherein he wont at Heaven's high council-table
To sit the midst of Trinal Unity,
He laid aside; and here with us to be,
    Forsook the courts of everlasting day,
And chose with us a darksome house of mortal
    clay.

John Milton (1608–1674)

I.

Lord Jesus,
you issued from the heart of the eternal Father
for us and for our salvation
and were conceived by the power of the Holy Spirit
in the womb of the humble Virgin Mary.

~WORD MADE FLESH, EMMANUEL OUR GOD,
HAVE MERCY ON US.

Lord Jesus,
during the visit of your mother, Mary,
to her cousin Elizabeth,
John the Baptist, your herald and forerunner,
was filled with the Holy Spirit,
and danced for joy in his mother's womb.

~WORD MADE FLESH, EMMANUEL OUR GOD,
HAVE MERCY ON US.

Lord Jesus,
though by nature divine,
you did not parade your equality with God,
but became a human being
and were enclosed for nine months in Mary's
     womb.

~WORD MADE FLESH, EMMANUEL OUR GOD,
HAVE MERCY ON US.

Lord Jesus,
born in Bethlehem, the City of David,
you were wrapped in swaddling clothes
and laid in a manger;
you were heralded by angelic choirs
and visited by wondering shepherds.

~WORD MADE FLESH, EMMANUEL OUR GOD,
HAVE MERCY ON US.

All glory, Jesus, be to you
Forevermore the Virgin's Son,
To Father and to Paraclete
Be praise while endless ages run!

Christ has drawn near to us, alleluia!
~COME, LET US ADORE OUR NEWBORN LORD,
ALLELUIA!

Let us pray:

Pour forth, O Lord,
your grace into our hearts,

that we to whom the incarnation of Christ
   your Son
was made known by the message of an angel,
may by his passion and cross
be brought to the glory of his resurrection;
through the same Christ our Lord.
~AMEN.

II.

Lord Jesus,
on the eighth day after your birth,
you were circumcised according to the law
of Moses,
and were given the holy name of Jesus,
the name revealed to Mary and Joseph
before his conception.

~WORD MADE FLESH, EMMANUEL OUR GOD,
HAVE MERCY ON US.

Lord Jesus,
by the leading of a star,
you were revealed to the Magi from the East,
who adored you on Mary's lap
and honored you with mystical gifts:
gold, frankincense, and myrrh.

~WORD MADE FLESH, EMMANUEL OUR GOD,
HAVE MERCY ON US.

Lord Jesus,
forty days after your birth,
your parents presented you in the temple,

where the aged Simeon and Anna recognized you
as the light of the Gentiles and the glory of Israel.

~WORD MADE FLESH, EMMANUEL OUR GOD,
HAVE MERCY ON US.

Lord Jesus,
after the visit of the Magi,
an angel appeared to Joseph in a dream
and warned him to flee to Egypt
with you and your mother,
to escape King Herod's fury.

~WORD MADE FLESH, EMMANUEL OUR GOD,
HAVE MERCY ON US.

All glory, Jesus, be to you
Forevermore the Virgin's Son,
To Father and to Paraclete
Be praise while endless ages run!

Christ is born for us, alleluia!

~COME, LET US ADORE HIM, ALLELUIA!

Let us pray:

Abba, dear Father,
by the fruitful virginity of the holy Virgin Mary,
you conferred on us the blessings of salvation.
Grant that we may experience the power of her
    intercession
through whom we received the Author of life,
Jesus Christ our Lord.

~AMEN.

III.

Lord Jesus,
your flight into Egypt snatched you
from a cruel death,
but a voice was heard in Ramah,
wailing and loud lamentation,
Rachel weeping for her children,
and refusing to be comforted,
because they were no more.

~WORD MADE FLESH, EMMANUEL OUR GOD,
HAVE MERCY ON US.

Lord Jesus,
after cruel Herod's death,
an angel again appeared to Joseph in a dream,
commanding him to take you and your mother
back to the land of Israel,
where you made your home in Nazareth of Galilee.

~WORD MADE FLESH, EMMANUEL OUR GOD,
HAVE MERCY ON US.

Lord Jesus,
in the humble home of Nazareth,
you lived in obedience to your parents,
and grew in wisdom and age
and in divine and human favor,
while your mother treasured all these things
in her heart.

~WORD MADE FLESH, EMMANUEL OUR GOD,
HAVE MERCY ON US.

Lord Jesus,
when you were twelve years old,
at Passover you lingered in Jerusalem;
and after three days your parents found you
in the temple,
sitting among the teachers of the Law,
listening to them and asking them questions.

~WORD MADE FLESH, EMMANUEL OUR GOD,
HAVE MERCY ON US.

All glory, Jesus, be to you
Forevermore the Virgin's son,
To Father and to Paraclete
Be praise while endless ages run!

The Word was made flesh, alleluia!
~AND CAME TO LIVE AMONG US, ALLELUIA!

Closing Prayer

Let us pray:

God of peace and consolation,
as we recall and worship
the mysteries of your Son's infancy and childhood,
may we be filled with the spirit of humility,
grow into the full stature of the children of God,
and come at last to our heavenly home
which you promise to your adopted children
    and heirs.
We ask this through the same Christ our Lord,
who lives and reigns with you and the Holy
    Spirit,

one God, now and forever.

~A<small>MEN</small>.[26]

December 31, Vigil of New Year's Day

"Popular Piety has given rise to many pious exercises connected with December 31."[27] The sentiments of penance and sorrow for past sins and thanksgiving for the blessings of the past year have given rise to Vigils or Watch Night services in church or home. They are often composed of appropriate songs and psalms, periods of silent reflection, the singing of the Te Deum, and the celebration of Mass. Such a service is often conducted for a half hour before midnight and a half hour after midnight. The following might serve for a New Year's vigil service.

In the name of the Father, † and of the Son, and of the Holy Spirit.

~A<small>MEN</small>.

Act of Contrition

Almighty and most merciful God,
you love all that you have created
and have pity on all that you have made.
In your overflowing loving-kindness,
blot out our offenses and cancel all our sins,
create clean hearts for us,
and put a steadfast spirit within us,
so that we may serve you in joy
and thank you with grateful hearts
all the days of our lives.

We ask this through Christ,
our blessed mediator and redeemer.
~Amen.

Psalm 117 Praise the Lord!

Leader: Holy is God, holy and strong, holy and living forever.

All: ~Holy is God, holy and strong, holy and living forever.

O praise the Lord, all you nations,
acclaim God all you peoples!

~Holy is God, holy and strong, holy and living forever.

Strong is God's love for us;
the Lord is faithful forever.

~Holy is God, holy and strong, holy and living forever.

Glory to the Father, and to the Son, and to the Holy Spirit:

~Holy is God, holy and strong, holy and living forever.
as it was in the beginning, is now, and will be forever. Amen.

~Holy is God, holy and strong, holy and living forever.

Psalm Prayer

Let us pray *(pause for quiet prayer)*:

Holy God and Father of us all,
the seraphim praise you,
the cherubim sing your glory,
and all the powers of heaven fall down
in adoration before you.
As we stand in your holy presence,
permit us to offer you the worship you deserve
in union with the holy Mother of God
and the whole company of heaven;
through the merits of Jesus Christ our Savior.
~Amen.

Reading Transformation Romans 12:1–2

I appeal to you, brothers and sisters, by the mercies of God, to present your bodies as a living sacrifice, holy and acceptable to God, which is your spiritual worship. Do not be conformed to this world, but be transformed by the renewing of your minds, so that you may discern what is the will of God— what is good and acceptable and perfect.

Silence

Response
Be holy, says the Lord,
~For I am holy.

The Song of the Church (Te Deum)[28]

A. We praise you, O God,
we acclaim you as Lord;
all creation worships you,
the Father everlasting.

To you all angels, all the powers of heaven,
the cherubim and seraphim, sing in endless praise:
  Holy, holy, holy Lord, God of power and
    might,
  heaven and earth are full of your glory.

The glorious company of apostles praise you.
The noble fellowship of prophets praise you.
The white-robed army of martyrs praise you.

Throughout the world the holy Church acclaims
    you:
  Father, of majesty unbounded,
  your true and only Son, worthy of all praise,
  and the Holy Spirit, advocate and guide.

B. You, Christ, are the king of glory,
the eternal Son of the Father.
When you took our flesh to set us free
you humbly chose the Virgin's womb.

You overcame the sting of death
and opened the kingdom of heaven to all believers.
You are seated at God's right hand in glory.
We believe that you will come to be our judge.

Come then, Lord, and help your people,
bought with the price of your own blood,
and bring us with your saints
to glory everlasting.

C. Save your people, Lord, and bless your
inheritance.
~GOVERN AND UPHOLD THEM NOW AND ALWAYS.

Day by day we bless you.
~WE PRAISE YOUR NAME FOR EVER.

Keep us today, Lord, from all sin.
~HAVE MERCY ON US, LORD, HAVE MERCY.

Lord, show us your love and mercy.
~FOR WE HAVE PUT OUR TRUST IN YOU.

In you, Lord, is our hope.
~LET US NEVER BE PUT TO SHAME.

General Thanksgiving
Almighty God, Father of all mercies,
we your unworthy servants give you humble thanks
for all your goodness and loving-kindness
to us and to all whom you have made.
We bless you for our creation, preservation,
and all the blessings of this life;
but above all for your immeasurable love
in the redemption of the world by our Lord Jesus
Christ;
for the means of grace and for the hope of glory.
And, we pray, give us such awareness of your
mercies,

that with truly thankful hearts we may show forth
    your praise,
not only with our lips, but in our lives,
by giving up ourselves to your service,
and by walking before you
in holiness and righteousness all our days;
through Jesus Christ our Lord,
to whom, with you and the Holy Spirit,
be honor and glory throughout all ages.
~Amen.[29]

Doxology

Blessing and honor and thanksgiving and praise
more than we can utter, more than we can conceive,
be yours, O holy and glorious Trinity,
Father, Son, and Holy Spirit,
by all angels, all human beings, all creatures,
forever and ever.
~Amen.

Bishop Thomas Ken (1631–1711)

January 1, Solemnity of the Mother of God and the Octave of Christmas

This is "an eminently Marian feast" by which "the
Church celebrates the divine and virginal motherhood
of the Mother of God: for our Lady it was the foretaste
and cause of her extraordinary glory; for us it is a
source of grace and salvation because through her we
have received the Author of life."[30]

A Devotion in Honor of the Virgin Mary

Blessed be the great Mother of God, Mary
most holy!

~BLESSED BE THE NAME OF MARY, VIRGIN AND
MOTHER!

A Marian Hymn

Mary the dawn, Christ the perfect Day.
Mary the gate, Christ the heavenly Way.

Mary the root, Christ the mystic Vine.
Mary the grape, Christ the sacred Wine.

Mary the wheat, Christ the living Bread.
Mary the rosebush, Christ the Rose bloodred.

Mary the font, Christ the cleansing Flood.
Mary the chalice, Christ the saving Blood.

Mary the temple, Christ the temple's Lord.
Mary the shrine, Christ the God adored.

Mary the beacon, Christ the haven's Rest.
Mary the mirror, Christ the Vision blest.

Mary the mother, Christ the mother's Son.
By all things blest while endless ages run.[31]

Psalm 113 God's Goodness

ANTIPHON HAIL, HOLY MOTHER!
THE CHILD TO WHOM YOU GAVE BIRTH
IS THE RULER OF HEAVEN AND EARTH, ALLELUIA!

Praise, O servants of the LORD,
praise the name of the LORD!

May the name of the LORD be blessed
both now and for evermore!
From the rising of the sun to its setting
praised be the name of the LORD!

High above all nations is the LORD,
above the heavens God's glory.
Who is like the LORD, our God,
the one enthroned on high,
who stoops from the heights to look down,
to look down upon heaven and earth?

From the dust God lifts up the lowly,
from the dungheap God raises the poor
to set them in the company of rulers,
yes, with the rulers of the people.
To the childless wife God gives a home
and gladdens her heart with children.

ANTIPHON HAIL, HOLY MOTHER!
THE CHILD TO WHOM YOU GAVE BIRTH
IS THE RULER OF HEAVEN AND EARTH, ALLELUIA!

Psalm Prayer

Let us pray *(pause for quiet prayer):*

Lord our God,
you have made the Virgin Mary
the model for all who welcome your word
and who put it into practice.
Open our hearts to receive it with joy
and by the power of your Spirit

grant that we also may become a dwelling place
in which your word of salvation is fulfilled.
We ask this through Christ our Lord.
~Amen.[32]

Reading Good News for Mary
Luke 1:35, 37–38

The angel said to her, "The Holy Spirit will come
upon you, and the power of the Most High will
overshadow you; therefore the child to be born
will be called Son of God. For nothing will be
impossible with God." Then Mary said, "Here am
I, the servant of the Lord; let it be with me
according to your word."

Silence

Response

Blessed are you among women, O Mary,
~And blessed is the fruit of your womb, Jesus.

Canticle of the Virgin Mary
Luke 1:46–55[33]

Antiphon The root of Jesse has flowered;
the star of Jacob has risen;
a Virgin has brought forth the Savior, alleluia!

My soul † proclaims the greatness of the Lord,
my spirit rejoices in God my Savior,
for you, Lord, have looked with favor on your
    lowly servant.

From this day all generations will call me blessed:
    you, the Almighty, have done great things for me
    and holy is your name.
    You have mercy on those who fear you,
    from generation to generation.

You have shown strength with your arm
and scattered the proud in their conceit,
casting down the mighty from their thrones
    and lifting up the lowly.
You have filled the hungry with good things
and sent the rich away empty.

You have come to the aid of your servant Israel,
to remember the promise of mercy,
the promise made to our forebears,
to Abraham and his children forever.

Glory to the Father, and to the Son,
and to the Holy Spirit:
as it was in the beginning, is now,
and will be forever. Amen.

ANTIPHON THE ROOT OF JESSE HAS FLOWERED;
THE STAR OF JACOB HAS RISEN;
A VIRGIN HAS BROUGHT FORTH THE SAVIOR,
ALLELUIA!

Litany of the Blessed Virgin Mary (see pages 221–223 or 223–225)

Closing Prayer

Blessed Savior,
we come before you in worship
to pay our vows at your shrine,
the glorious Virgin's lap,
where you are enthroned for our adoration.
Here we pray for ourselves,
and for the whole world besides,
and especially for the poor and afflicted,
the desolate and deprived peoples of the earth.
Blessed are you, O Christ, now and forever.
~AMEN.

May the Virgin Mother mild
✝ bless us with her holy Child.
~AMEN.

Besides marking the beginning of the civil year, January 1 has also been designated since 1967 as the Day of Prayer for World Peace. This designation has given rise "to intense prayer for world peace, education for peace, education towards peace and those values inextricably linked with it, such as liberty, fraternal solidarity, the dignity of the human person, respect for nature, the right to work, the sacredness of human life, and the denunciation of human injustices."[34]

Epiphany, the Baptism of the Lord, and the Presentation

Jesus was first made known to the shepherds of Bethlehem by the ministry of singing angels. The shepherds, in turn, announced what they had experienced to their friends and neighbors, "and all who heard it were amazed at what the shepherds told them" (Luke 2:18). Some time later, wise men, led by a star, came from the East to Jerusalem and then to Bethlehem, looking for the newborn king of the Jews. Their precious gifts signified Jesus' mission and coming death and opened the gentile world to the gospel.

But these two epiphanies (revelations) were only the beginning. Next came Jesus' presentation in the temple of Jerusalem and his manifestation to the two holy prophets, old Simeon and the aged Anna, who represented "all who were looking for the redemption of Israel" (Luke 2:38). Then there came the baptism of Jesus by John the Baptist, inaugurating the messianic age and his public ministry in Galilee and Judea. Finally, there was the revelation of Jesus' glory to his first disciples at the wedding feast of Cana.

In the Liturgy and in popular piety Christmas and the Presentation of the Lord maintain their fixed feast days on December 25 and February 2. But the Epiphany and the Baptism of the Lord are now observed on the Lord's Day in Canada and the United States: the Feast of the Epiphany is celebrated on the first Sunday after January 1, and the Baptism of Our Lord on the Sunday next.

In families, the Epiphany may include an exchange of simple gifts, the blessing of the home with the writing of the initials of the three Magi on its lintel (C+M+B), and an Epiphany cake with three small crowns or coins buried in it. The Feast of the Presentation is closely associated with the annual blessing of candles for church and home (Candlemas) and as a sign of Christ, the Light of the world.[35]

Devotion for Epiphany, Baptism, and Presentation

You are the bright and the morning star,
~O CHRIST OUR LORD.

We observed his star at its rising
~AND HAVE COME TO PAY HIM HOMAGE.

You are my Son, the Beloved;
~WITH YOU I AM WELL PLEASED.

A light of revelation to the gentiles
~AND THE GLORY OF YOUR PEOPLE ISRAEL.

AN EPIPHANY HYMN

When Christ was born, God sent a star,
A sign of hope whence light should spring,
And Israel's glory shine for all,
For pagan and for pilgrim-king.

He is the Father's only Son
On whom the Spirit came to rest,
Who was baptized to cleanse our sins:
The Lamb of God and Savior blest.

He is the anchor of our soul
And shares with us his life divine;
For sadness he exchanges joy,
As water he once changed to wine.

We praise the Father, Lord of life,
And Christ, his well-beloved Son,
Who with the Spirit is our peace:
Most tranquil Trinity in One.[36]

PSALM 2   GOD PROCLAIMS THE ANOINTED SON

ANTIPHON YOU ARE MY SON. IT IS I WHO HAVE
BEGOTTEN YOU THIS DAY.

Why this tumult among nations,
among peoples this useless murmuring?
They arise, the kings of the earth,
princes plot against the LORD and his Anointed.
"Come, let us break their fetters,
come, let us cast off their yoke."

God who sits in the heavens laughs,
the Lord is laughing them to scorn.
Then God will speak in anger,
and in rage will strike them in terror.
"It is I who have set up my king,
on Zion, my holy mountain."

The Lord said to me: "You are my Son.
It is I who have begotten you this day.
Ask and I shall bequeath you the nations,
put the ends of the earth in your possession.
With a rod of iron you will break them,
shatter them like a potter's jar."

Now, O kings, understand,
take warning, rulers of the earth;
serve the LORD with awe
and trembling, pay your homage
lest God be angry and you perish;
for suddenly God's anger will blaze.

Blessed are they who put their trust in God.

ANTIPHON YOU ARE MY SON. IT IS I WHO HAVE BEGOTTEN YOU THIS DAY.

PSALM PRAYER

Let us pray *(pause for quiet prayer):*

Jesus, anointed Son of God,
Daystar from on high and Prince of Peace,
fill the world with your splendor,
shelter us from tyrants and exploiters
and show the nations the light of truth.
You live and reign, now and forever.
~AMEN.

READINGS

EPIPHANY   **GOD'S TRUE IMAGE**   **HEBREWS 1:1–3**[37]

In the past God spoke to our ancestors many times and in many ways through the prophets, but in these last days he has spoken to us through his Son. He is the one through whom God created the universe, the one whom God has chosen to possess all things at the end. He reflects the brightness of God's glory and is the exact likeness of God's own being, sustaining the universe with his powerful word. After achieving forgiveness for human sins, he sat down in heaven at the right-hand side of God, the Supreme Power.

SILENCE

RESPONSE

The Lord has made known salvation, alleluia!

BAPTISM   THE WORD OF LIFE   1 JOHN 1:1–3[38]

We write to you about the Word of life, which has existed from the very beginning. We have heard it, and we have seen it with our eyes; yes, we have seen it, and our hands have touched it. When this life became visible, we saw it; so we speak of it and tell you about the eternal life which was with the Father and was made known to us. What we have seen and heard we announce to you also, so that you will join with us in the fellowship that we have with the Father and with his Son Jesus Christ.

SILENCE

RESPONSE

Prepare the way of the Lord, alleluia!

~MAKE HIS PATHS STRAIGHT, ALLELUIA!

PRESENTATION   SIMEON AND ANNA   LUKE 2:27–28, 36, 38, 33

Guided by the Spirit, Simeon came into the temple; and when the parents brought in the child Jesus, to do for him what was customary under the law, Simeon took him in his arms and praised God. There was also a prophet, Anna. At that moment she came, and began to praise God and to speak about the child to all who were looking for the redemption of Jerusalem. And the

child's father and mother were amazed at what
was being said about him.

SILENCE

RESPONSE

My eyes have seen your salvation, alleluia!
~WHICH YOU HAVE PREPARED IN THE SIGHT OF ALL
PEOPLES, ALLELUIA!

CANTICLE OF THE WORD　　**JOHN 1:1–5, 10–12, 14**
ANTIPHONS
Epiphany
This is a holy time adorned with three mysteries:
A STAR LEADS THE MAGI TO THE MANGER,
WATER IS MADE WINE AT THE WEDDING OF CANA,
AND CHRIST IS BAPTIZED BY JOHN IN THE JORDAN
IN ORDER TO SAVE US, ALLELUIA!

Baptism
You are my Son, the Beloved;
WITH YOU I AM WELL PLEASED.

Presentation
Christ is the light of the nations, alleluia!
AND THE GLORY OF ISRAEL HIS PEOPLE, ALLELUIA!

In the beginning was the Word,
and the Word was with God,
and the Word was God.
He was in the beginning with God.

All things came into being through him,

and without him not one thing came into being.
What has come into being in him was life,
and the life was the light of all people.
The light shines in the darkness,
and the darkness did not overcome it.

He was in the world,
and the world came into being through him;
yet the world did not know him.
He came to what was his own,
and his own people did not accept him.
But to all who received him,
who believed in his name,
he gave power to become children of God.

And the Word became flesh
and lived among us,
and we have seen his glory,
the glory as of a father's only son,
full of grace and truth.

Glory to the Father, and to the Son,
and to the Holy Spirit:
as it was in the beginning, is now,
and will be forever. Amen.

(The proper antiphon is repeated.)

LITANY

By the sacred mysteries of the Word made flesh,
> let us pray to the Lord.

~LORD, HAVE MERCY.

By the wondrous birth in time of the timeless Son
of God, let us pray to the Lord.
~LORD, HAVE MERCY.

By the humble nativity of the King of glory
in the stable of Bethlehem,
let us pray to the Lord.
~LORD, HAVE MERCY.

By the splendid manifestation of the king of the
Jews to the shepherds and the Magi,
let us pray to the Lord.
~LORD, HAVE MERCY.

By the meeting with old Simeon and Anna
when Jesus first visited the temple,
let us pray to the Lord.
~LORD, HAVE MERCY.

By the lowly submission of the Maker of the
world to Mary and Joseph of Nazareth,
let us pray to the Lord.
~LORD, HAVE MERCY.

By the holy baptism of the beloved Son of God
by John in the Jordan, let us pray to the Lord.
~LORD, HAVE MERCY.

By the revealing miracle of the water made wine
at Cana in Galilee,
let us pray to the Lord.
~LORD, HAVE MERCY.

For the conversion of the whole human race to
     our Savior Jesus Christ,
     let us pray to the Lord.
~LORD, HAVE MERCY.[39]

(Pause for special intentions.)

In the communion with the great Mother of God,
Mary most holy, St. Joseph her spouse, St. John
the Baptist, and with all the saints, let us
commend ourselves, one another, and our whole
life to Christ our Lord.
~TO YOU, O LORD.

THE LORD'S PRAYER

CLOSING PRAYERS
Epiphany
Father of light, unchanging God,
you reveal to those of faith
the resplendent fact of the Word made flesh.
Your light is strong, your love is near;
draw us beyond the limits which this world
     imposes
to the life where the Spirit makes all life complete.
We ask this through Christ our Lord.
~AMEN.[40]

Baptism

God of power and life,
glory of all who believe in you
fill the world with your splendor
and show the nations the light of your truth;
through Jesus Christ our Lord.
~AMEN.

Presentation

All-powerful Father,
Christ your Son became man for us
and was presented in the temple.
May he free our hearts from sin
and bring us into your presence,
where he lives and reigns with you
and the Holy Spirit, one God,
now and forever.
~AMEN.[41]

May Christ, the Word of God,
the life and light of the world,
✝ bless us and keep us.
~AMEN.

The Season of Lent

Lent is a season of final preparation for those about to be baptized during the Easter Vigil. It is also a time for those already baptized to repent of sins they have committed since their baptism, approach the sacrament of reconciliation, and renew their baptismal vows at the vigil.

Traditionally, Lent calls—in a special way—for three observances: prayer, fasting, and almsgiving: *prayer* to fix the mind on Christ and the gospel message; *fasting* to help the body share in the sufferings of Jesus and of the poor; and *almsgiving* to set aside money for those in need. Almsgiving includes gifts of time and money and commitment to the corporal and spiritual works of mercy.

What exactly are the corporal and spiritual works of mercy? The corporal works of mercy are to feed the hungry, give drink to the thirsty, clothe the naked, shelter the homeless, visit the sick, visit prisoners, and bury the dead. The spiritual works of mercy are to counsel the doubtful, instruct the ignorant, admonish sinners, comfort the afflicted, forgive offenses, bear wrongs patiently, and pray for the living and the dead.

In popular devotion, Lent is an anticipation of the Holy Week and the paschal Triduum and often uses the way of the cross on Fridays, concentrates on the sorrowful mysteries of the rosary, and prays the *Stabat Mater.* (See pages 132–134.)

Lenten Meal Prayers

Before Dinner

LEADER: Repent and believe in the Good News.
ALL: ~THE KINGDOM OF GOD IS AT HAND.

LEADER: Heavenly Father,
each year you purify your Church
by the observance of Lent.
Help us in our preparation for Easter,
wash us clean from all our sins,
and show us how to combine
self-denial and good deeds.
We ask this through Christ our Lord.
ALL: ~AMEN.

LEADER: Lord, have mercy.
ALL: CHRIST, HAVE MERCY. LORD, HAVE MERCY.

LEADER: Our Father . . . *(Continue in unison.)*

LEADER: Bless ✝ us, O Lord, and these your gifts
which we are about to receive from your bounty;
through Christ our Lord.
ALL: ~AMEN.

LEADER: May the King of eternal glory
make us sit at his welcome table in heaven.
ALL: ~AMEN.

After Dinner

LEADER: Seek the Lord, who is still to be found.

ALL: ~CALL UPON GOD, WHO IS YET AT HAND.

LEADER: Lord Jesus Christ,
you loved us and delivered yourself up for us
as an agreeable and fragrant sacrifice to God.
Rescue us from our former darkness
and teach us to live as children of the light
in all goodness, justice, and truth.
You live and reign forever and ever.

ALL: ~AMEN.

LEADER: Almighty God,
we give you thanks for these and for all your gifts.
You live and reign forever and ever.

ALL: ~AMEN.

LEADER: Reward with eternal life, O Lord,
all those who do us good for your name's sake.

ALL: ~AMEN.

LEADER: May the souls of the faithful departed
through the mercy of God rest in peace.

ALL: ~AMEN.

Daily Devotions during Lent

In the name of the Father, † and of the Son,
and of the Holy Spirit.

~AMEN.

Worship the Lord in the beauty of holiness;
~Tremble before God, all the earth.

For the Lord is coming;
~He is coming to judge all creatures.

Hymn of Repentance
King high exalted,
all the world's Redeemer,
to you your children
lift their eyes with weeping;
Christ, we implore you,
hear our supplications.

Right hand of Godhead,
headstone of the corner,
path of salvation,
gate to heaven's kingdom,
cleanse your sinful people
stained with transgressions.

On our knees before you,
Majesty eternal,
we lament our sinfulness
in your holy hearing.

Humbly now confessing,
countless sins admitting,
we lay bare our secrets;
may your boundless mercy
grant to us full pardon.

Captive led away,
guiltless, unresisting,
charged by false witness,
unto death for sinners,
Jesus Christ protect us
whom your blood has purchased.[42]

PSALM 51   A PLEA FOR FORGIVENESS

ANTIPHON   IF WE DIE WITH THE LORD,
WE SHALL LIVE WITH THE LORD.

Have mercy on me, God, in your kindness.
In your compassion blot out my offense.
O wash me more and more from my guilt
and cleanse me from my sin.

My offenses, truly I know them;
my sin is always before me.
Against you, you alone, have I sinned;
what is evil in your sight I have done.

That you may be justified when you give sentence
and be without reproach when you judge.
O see, in guilt I was born;
O wash me, I shall be whiter than snow.

Make me hear rejoicing and gladness
that the bones you have crushed may revive.
From my sin turn away your face
and blot out all my guilt.

A pure heart create for me, O God,
put a steadfast spirit within me.
Do not cast me away from your presence,
nor deprive me of your holy spirit.

Give me again the joy of your help;
with a spirit of fervor sustain me,
that I may teach transgressors your ways
and sinners may return to you.

O rescue me, God, my helper,
and my tongue shall ring out your goodness.
O Lord, open my lips
and my mouth shall declare your praise.

For in sacrifice you take no delight,
burnt offering from me you would refuse;
my sacrifice, a contrite spirit,
a humbled, contrite heart you will not spurn.[43]

ANTIPHON IF WE DIE WITH THE LORD,
WE SHALL LIVE WITH THE LORD.

PSALM PRAYER

Let us pray *(pause for quiet prayer):*

Abba, gracious Father,
when David repented before you
in sackcloth and ashes,
you poured out on him
the healing medicine of your forgiveness.
By following David's example
may we reshape our hearts,
enter into your wisdom,
and offer you gifts that please you.
We make our prayer through Jesus our Savior.
~AMEN.

READING   DRY BONES   EZEKIEL 37:4–6[44]

The LORD said to Ezekiel: "Prophesy to the bones.
Tell these dry bones to listen to the word of the
LORD. Tell them that I, the Sovereign LORD, am
saying to them: I am going to put breath into you
and bring you back to life. I will give you sinews
and muscles, and cover you with skin. I will put
breath into you and bring you back to life. Then
you will know that I am the LORD."

SILENCE

RESPONSE

I will put my breath in them
~AND BRING THEM BACK TO LIFE.

OR THIS READING   THE BEATITUDES   LUKE 6:20–26

Jesus looked up at his disciples and said:

"Blessed are you who are poor,
for yours is the kingdom of God.
Blessed are you who are hungry now,
for you will be filled.
Blessed are you who weep now,
for you will laugh.
Blessed are you when people hate you,
and when they exclude you,
revile you, and defame you
on account of the Son of Man.
Rejoice in that day and leap for joy,
for surely your reward is great in heaven;

for that is what their ancestors did
　　to the prophets.

But woe to you who are rich,
for you have received your consolation.
Woe to you who are full now,
for you will be hungry.
Woe to you who are laughing now,
for you will mourn and weep.
Woe to you when all speak well of you,
for that is what their ancestors did
　　to the false prophets."

SILENCE

RESPONSE
The Lord does not seek the death of sinners,
~BUT RATHER THAT THEY BE CONVERTED AND LIVE.

CANTICLE OF JEREMIAH THE PROPHET (7:2–7)[45]
ANTIPHON　MY THOUGHTS ARE NOT YOUR THOUGHTS,
SAYS THE LORD.

Change the way you are living
and the things you are doing
and I will let you go on living here.

Stop believing those deceitful words,
"We are safe!
This is the LORD's Temple
this is the LORD's Temple,
this is the LORD's Temple!"

Change the way you are living
and stop doing the things you are doing.
Be fair in your treatment of one another.
Stop taking advantage of aliens, orphans, and
    widows.
Stop killing innocent people in this land.
Stop worshipping other gods,
for that will destroy you.

If you change, I will let you go on living here
in the land which I gave your ancestors
as a permanent possession.

Glory to the Father, and to the Son,
and to the Holy Spirit:
as it was in the beginning, is now,
and will be forever. Amen.

ANTIPHON MY THOUGHTS ARE NOT YOUR THOUGHTS,
SAYS THE LORD.

LITANY

For the peace of Christ in the reign of Christ:
~LORD, HEAR OUR PRAYER.

For true faith and undying hope:
~LORD, HEAR OUR PRAYER.

For neighborly concern and true affection:
~LORD, HEAR OUR PRAYER.

For those who need our care and assistance:
~LORD, HEAR OUR PRAYER.

For the heavily burdened and afflicted:
~LORD, HEAR OUR PRAYER.

For the mentally handicapped and diseased:
~LORD, HEAR OUR PRAYER.

For the friendless and abandoned:
~LORD, HEAR OUR PRAYER.

For our beloved dead who died in the Lord:
~LORD, HEAR OUR PRAYER.

(Pause for special intentions.)

By the prayers of the Blessed Virgin Mary
   and of the whole company of heaven:
~LORD, HEAR OUR PRAYER.

THE LORD'S PRAYER

CLOSING PRAYER
Lord Jesus Christ,
you descended into the womb of the Virgin
and ascended the wood of the Cross
for our salvation.
By our Lenten observances
of prayer, fasting, and almsgiving,
teach us true self-denial
and genuine attachment to your holy will for us.
You live and reign forever and ever.
~AMEN.

May the Lord bless us and take care of us;
May the Lord be kind and gracious to us;

May the Lord look on us with favor
and † give us peace.
~Amen.

A Devotion to the Five Wounds of Jesus Crucified

Our forebears in the faith saw in the five wounds of Jesus on the cross the indelible signs of God's love for us in Christ. They instituted numerous devotions to the five wounds of our Savior as they cried out in prayer with Thomas the Apostle, "My Lord and my God!" (John 20:28).

In the name of the Father, † and of the Son,
and of the Holy Spirit.
~Amen.
They tear holes in my hands and my feet
~And lay me in the dust of death.

Hymn   **The Blessed Passion**

O love, how deep, how broad, how high,
How passing thought and fantasy,
That God, the Son of God should take
Our mortal form for mortals' sake.

For us to evil power betrayed,
Scourged, mocked, in purple robe arrayed,
He bore the shameful cross and death,
For us gave up his dying breath.

For us he rose from death again;
For us he went on high to reign;

For us he sent the Spirit here
To guide, to strengthen, and to cheer.

All glory to our Lord and God
For love so deep, so high, so broad:
The Trinity whom we adore
Forever and forevermore.

Attributed to Thomas à Kempis (fifteenth century),
trans. John Mason Neale (1851)

PSALM 16   JESUS CRIES OUT TO HIS FATHER

ANTIPHON LET US PRAISE CHRIST
WHO WAS PIERCED WITH FIVE PRECIOUS WOUNDS.

Preserve me, God, I take refuge in you.
I say to you, LORD: "You are my God.
My happiness lies in you alone."

You have put into my heart a marvelous love
for the faithful ones who dwell in your land.
Those who choose other gods increase their sorrows.
Never will I offer their offerings of blood.
Never will I take their name upon my lips.

O LORD, it is you who are my portion and cup,
it is you yourself who are my prize.
The lot marked out for me is my delight,
welcome indeed the heritage that falls to me!

I will bless you, LORD, you give me counsel,
and even at night direct my heart.
I keep you, LORD, ever in my sight;
since you are at my right hand, I shall stand firm.

And so my heart rejoices, my soul is glad;
even my body shall rest in safety.
For you will not leave my soul among the dead,
nor let your beloved know decay.

You will show me the path of life,
the fullness of joy in your presence,
at your right hand happiness forever.

ANTIPHON LET US PRAISE CHRIST, WHO WAS PIERCED
WITH FIVE PRECIOUS WOUNDS.

PSALM PRAYER
Let us pray *(pause for quiet prayer):*

Lord Jesus crucified,
we kiss your five priceless wounds,
indelible marks of love made visible.
You begged your Father for help
when you were wounded and surrounded by
    enemies.
We now implore you to come to our assistance
and be our precious Savior,
now and forever.
~AMEN.

JESUS LIFTED UP
READING ON THE CROSS JOHN 3:14–17

Jesus said, "Just as Moses lifted up the serpent in
the wilderness, so must the Son of Man be lifted
up, that whoever believes in him may have eternal
life. For God so loved the world that he gave his

only Son, so that everyone who believes in him
may not perish but may have eternal life. Indeed,
God did not send the Son into the world to con-
demn the world, but in order that the world might
be saved through him."

SILENCE

RESPONSE

We adore you, O Christ, and we bless you,
~FOR BY YOUR HOLY CROSS YOU HAVE REDEEMED
THE WORLD.

CANTICLE OF THE
 ## LAMB OF GOD   REVELATION 4:11; 5:9–10, 12
ANTIPHON THE BLOOD OF JESUS, GOD'S SON,
CLEANSES US FROM ALL SIN.

You are worthy, our Lord and God,
to receive glory and honor and power,
for you created all things,
and by your will they existed and were created.

You are worthy, O Christ,
to take the scroll and to open its seals,
for you were slaughtered
and by your blood you ransomed for God
saints from every tribe and language and people
    and nation;
you have made them to be a kingdom and priests
    serving our God,
and they will reign on earth.

Worthy is the Lamb that was slaughtered
to receive power and wealth and wisdom and might
and honor and glory and blessing.

ANTIPHON THE BLOOD OF JESUS, GOD'S SON,
CLEANSES US FROM ALL SIN.

LITANY OF THE LIFE-GIVING CROSS

Jesus, our blessed Savior, you embraced
   the bitter passion for us and our salvation:
~LORD, HAVE MERCY.

Friend of the human race, you accepted the cross
   and your five painful wounds for us:
~LORD, HAVE MERCY.

Man of Sorrows, the wicked tore holes in your
   hands and feet
   and laid you in the dust of death:
~LORD, HAVE MERCY.

Your beauty was marred to give us back the
   splendor of God:
~LORD, HAVE MERCY.

By your five holy wounds you vanquished hell
   and put dark death to flight:
~LORD, HAVE MERCY.

By your piteous death on the cross
   we are delivered from death and decay:
~LORD, HAVE MERCY.

(Pause for spontaneous prayer.)

By the prayers of the Mother of Sorrows
   and of all the martyrs and saints:
~LORD, HAVE MERCY.

CLOSING PRAYER

Father of your only-begotten Son,
in Jesus you give us everything we need.
As we venerate his five precious wounds,
may we share in all the blessings they bring us.
Be praised and thanked for your loving-kindness
to us and to all who worship the passion,
death, and resurrection of our blessed Savior,
who lives and reigns with you and the Holy Spirit,
now and forever.
~AMEN.

By his holy and glorious wounds
may Christ Jesus ✝ protect us and keep us.
~AMEN.

Another Devotion in Honor of the Five Wounds

This devotion to the Five Wounds is attributed to St. Clare of Assisi (1194–1253), the ardent and perfect disciple of St. Francis, the poor little man of Assisi (1181–1226). Towards the end of his life Francis had a vision of Christ crucified, and through that mystical experience he received both nails and wounds in his hands and feet and was pierced in his side. Francis was the first to receive these stigmata, as they are called, and as a kind of living crucifix he inspired fresh devotion to the cross and the five wounds of the

Savior. The three orders founded by St. Francis have been privileged to preach devotion to the sufferings of Jesus throughout the world for the last eight centuries.

IN HONOR OF THE WOUND IN HIS RIGHT HAND

Praise and glory to you, Lord Jesus,
for the wound in your right hand.
Through this wound of love,
please forgive all the sins I have committed
in thought, word, and deed,
by neglect of your service,
and by my self-indulgence
both waking and sleeping.
Help me to keep your death on the cross
and your five wounds always before my mind.
I want to show my gratitude to you
by carrying my own cross each day for your sake.
Please grant this, Lord Jesus,
you who live and reign, now and forever.
~AMEN.

IN HONOR OF THE WOUND IN HIS LEFT HAND

Praise and glory to you, Lord Jesus,
for the wound in your left hand.
Through this wound of love,
have mercy on me and remove from my heart
anything that displeases you.
Grant me victory over the restless enemy
that prowls about seeking to devour me.
Fill me with your strength
so that I may resist him, steadfast in faith.

The Season of Lent **85**

Through your merciful death
deliver me from all the dangers
that threaten my life and salvation
and make me become worthy of residing
in your heavenly home,
where you live and reign, now and forever.
~AMEN.

IN HONOR OF THE WOUND IN HIS RIGHT FOOT

Praise and glory to you, Jesus, good Savior,
for the holy wound in your right foot.
Through this wound of love,
grant that I may truly repent
in proportion to the magnitude of my sins.
Through your bitter death on the cross,
keep us continually united to your will
and preserve us body and soul from all adversity.
When the dread day of judgment comes,
receive my soul into your loving arms
and grant me eternal joy, O Lord,
you who live and reign, now and forever.
~AMEN.

IN HONOR OF THE WOUND IN HIS LEFT FOOT

Praise and glory to you, Lord Jesus,
for the wound in your left foot.
Through this wound of love,
please grant me full pardon of all my sins
so that before I die I may confess all my sins
with perfect contrition,

receive the sacrament of your Body and Blood,
be anointed for glory, and pass on to you
in complete purity of body and mind.
Hear my prayer, O Lord,
you who live and reign, now and forever.
~Amen.

In Honor of the Wound in His Side

Praise and glory to you, Jesus,
worthy of all love,
for the wound in your holy side.
Through this wound of love,
we see your immense mercy revealed,
not only to the Roman soldier
who pierced your heart,
but to us all.
I am now being delivered from every evil,
past, present, and yet to come,
through the merits of your precious blood
offered and received throughout the world.
By your bitter death,
please grant me lively faith,
unshakable hope, and perfect charity,
so that I may love you with all my heart
and mind and strength
and my neighbor as myself.
Establish me in your holy ways,
so that I may persevere in your service
and please you, both now and always.
~Amen.

A Devotion to the Precious Blood of Christ

If the five wounds of Jesus are the great signs of God's love for us, the precious blood of Jesus—poured out at his circumcision, at his flogging by Pilate, at his crowning with a wreath of thorns, at his bloodstained path to Golgotha, at his nailing to the cross, by his pierced side—is an even more vivid depiction and sign of God's undying love for us.

The renowned mystic Blessed Julian of Norwich (c. 1342–1423) helps us contemplate Jesus crucified and the efficacy of his precious blood:

> *The precious blood of our Lord Jesus Christ, as truly as it is most precious, so truly is it most plentiful. Behold and see the power of this most precious plenty of his precious blood. It descended into hell and broke its bonds, and delivered all who were there and who belong to the court of heaven. The precious plenty of his precious blood overflows all the earth and is ready to wash from their sins all creatures who are, have been, and will be of good will. The precious plenty of his precious blood ascended into heaven in the blessed body of our Lord Jesus Christ, and it is flowing there in him, praying to the Father for us, and this is and will be so long as we have need. And furthermore, it flows in all heaven, rejoicing in the salvation of all humankind which is and will be there, and filling up the number which is lacking.*[46]

In the name of the Father, ✝ and of the Son, and of the Holy Spirit.

~AMEN.

Blessed be the most precious blood of Jesus.

~BLESSED BE JESUS IN THE MOST HOLY SACRAMENT
OF THE ALTAR.

HYMN **WHEN I SURVEY THE WONDROUS CROSS
(INSPIRED BY GALATIANS 6:14)**

When I survey the wondrous Cross
on which the Prince of Glory died,
my richest gain I count but loss,
and pour contempt on all my pride.

Forbid it, Lord, that I should boast
save in the death of Christ, my God;
all the vain things that charm me most,
I sacrifice them to his blood.

See from his head, his hands, his feet,
sorrow and love flow mingled down;
did e'er such love and sorrow meet?
or thorns compose so rich a crown?

His dying crimson like a robe
spreads o'er his body on the Tree,
then am I dead to all the globe,
and all the globe is dead to me.

Were the whole realm of nature mine,
that were a present far too small;
love so amazing, so divine,
demands my soul, my life, my all.

Isaac Watts (1674–1748), alt.

ANTIPHON MAY THE GLORY OF YOUR BLOOD, O GOD,
SHINE ON EARTH!

Have mercy on me, God, have mercy
for in you my soul has taken refuge.
In the shadow of your wings I take refuge
till the storms of destruction pass by.

I call to you, God the Most High,
to you who have always been my help.
May you send from heaven and save me
and shame those who assail me.

My soul lies down among lions,
who would devour us, one and all.
Their teeth are spears and arrows,
their tongue a sharpened sword.

O God, arise above the heavens;
may your glory shine on earth!

They laid a snare for my steps,
my soul was bowed down.
They dug a pit in my path
but fell in it themselves.

My heart is ready, O God,
my heart is ready.
I will sing, I will sing your praise.
Awake, my soul;
awake, harp and lyre,
I will awake the dawn.

I will thank you, Lord, among the peoples,
among the nations I will praise you
for your love reaches to the heavens
and your truth to the skies.

ANTIPHON MAY THE GLORY OF YOUR BLOOD, O GOD,
SHINE ON EARTH!

PRAYER

Let us pray *(pause for quiet prayer)*:

God of love,
by Christ's blood we were redeemed
and our sins forgiven.
By the power of that same precious blood
defend us against all the evils of this life,
making peace by the blood of his cross.
In Jesus' name we ask it.
~AMEN.

HIGH PRIEST OF
READING THE NEW COVENANT   HEBREWS 10:19–22

My friends, since we have confidence to enter the
sanctuary by the blood of Jesus, by the new and
living way that he opened for us through the curtain (that is, through his flesh), and since we have a
great priest over the house of God, let us approach
with a true heart in full assurance of faith, with
our hearts sprinkled clean from an evil conscience.

SILENCE

RESPONSE

Come, Lord, and help your people,

~BOUGHT WITH THE PRICE OF YOUR OWN BLOOD.

**CANTICLE OF THE
  LAMB OF GOD**   REVELATION 4:11; 5:9–10, 12

ANTIPHON THE BLOOD OF JESUS, GOD'S SON,
CLEANSES US FROM ALL SIN.

You are worthy, our Lord and God,
to receive glory and honor and power,
for you created all things,
and by your will they existed and were created.

You are worthy, O Christ,
to take the scroll and to open its seals,
for you were slaughtered
and by your blood you ransomed for God
saints from every tribe and language and people
    and nation;
you have made them to be a kingdom and priests
    serving our God,
and they will reign on earth.

Worthy is the Lamb that was slaughtered
to receive power and wealth and wisdom and might
and honor and glory and blessing.

ANTIPHON THE BLOOD OF JESUS, GOD'S SON,
CLEANSES US FROM ALL SIN.

**LITANY OF THE PRECIOUS BLOOD OF JESUS
(SEE PAGES 217–218)**

CLOSING PRAYER

Lord Jesus,
lover of the whole human race,
you shed your precious blood for us on the cross
and renew this offering without ceasing on our
    altars
for us and for our salvation.
Remember us in all our needs,
save us from the time of trial
and deliver us from the evil one.
You live and reign, now and forever.
~Amen.

May the precious plenty of Christ's precious blood
✝ wash us from all sin.
~Amen.

A Devotion to the Sacred Heart of Jesus (see pages 206–211)

The Fifteen O's

This anonymous devotion to the passion of Jesus appeared in Latin in fourteenth-century England. It was soon translated into Middle English and circulated in manuscript and later in print in the fifteenth and later centuries. It is essentially a meditation on the various sufferings of Jesus from the judgment of Pilate to our Lord's death and burial. Coupled with the contemplation of his bitter passion are the seven words Jesus uttered as he was dying, another late-medieval devotion that has lasted through the centuries.

The Season of Lent **93**

Consideration of the wounds and lacerations of Christ, his degrees of suffering, and his seven last words is intimately connected with pleas for the forgiveness of sins through repentance and a devout reception of the holy sacraments. This devotion may also be used as a novena, since it contains many pleas for the things spiritual and temporal we need.

1. O Jesus, endless delight of those who love you,
joy surpassing all gladness and desire,
tender lover of repentant sinners,
you were pleased to come and dwell among us,
as you yourself declared.
Be mindful, blessed Jesus, of all the sorrows
you suffered during your sacred passion,
which was ordained by the Holy Trinity
for the salvation of the human race.
Remember, blessed Jesus, all the anguish and
   sorrow
you endured in your tender body before your
   crucifixion:
as you prayed with great tears in the Garden of
   Gethsemane,
were betrayed by Judas with a kiss,
arrested by a crowd with swords and clubs,
deserted by all your disciples,
denied by Peter in the courtyard of the high priest,
and testified against by false witnesses.
Remember that at Passover in Jerusalem,
in the flowering of your youth,
without any sin on your part,

you were condemned by Pilate to die on the cross,
were stripped of your clothes,
flogged, crowned with thorns,
mocked, scorned, spat upon, slapped,
and crushed with pain and humiliation.
Mindful of your blessed sufferings,
I entreat you, kind Jesus, to give me before I die
true contrition, complete confession,
and full remission of all my sins. Amen.

2. O Blessed Jesus, creator of the whole universe,
whom the whole world cannot contain,
be mindful of your bitter sorrows on the cross.
The soldiers of Pilate nailed your holy hands
and your tender feet to the cross
because you would not walk in their ways.
Then they lifted you up on the cross of agony
and joked and gambled by it
while your bright blood fell in great drops
and soaked into the ground.
In memory of your long, drawn-out pains on
    the cross,
I implore you, kind Jesus, to give me the grace
both to stand in awe of you
and to love you with all my heart.
Amen.

3. O Jesus, heavenly physician,
recall your exhaustion as the hours passed,
the blue-blackness of your five wounds,

as your once ruddy body shrank into death.
No sorrow was like your sorrow
for there was not a sound place in you
from the soles of your feet to the crown of your
 head.
And yet, forgetting all your grievous pains,
you prayed devoutly and charitably for your
 enemies,
*"Father, forgive them, for they know not what
 they do."*
For this loving mercy you showed your enemies
and for remembrance of these bitter pains,
may the memory of your blessed passion
become for me plenary remission and forgiveness
 of my sins.
Amen.

4. O Jesus, paradise of all spiritual delights,
recall the hideous dread that you suffered
when all your enemies gathered about your cross,
mocking, deriding, and taunting you.
In memory of these spiteful words
and of your sharp torments of body and mind,
I implore you, blessed Jesus,
deliver me from all my bodily and spiritual enemies
and set me under the wings of your blessed cross.
Amen.

5. O Jesus, blessed mirror of God's brightness,
remember that from all eternity
you beheld the chosen souls

who were predestined for salvation
by the merits of your passion.
Be mindful of your great mercy
you had towards us, lost and desperate sinners,
and especially for the great mercy which you
    showed
the repentant brigand who hung at your right
    side,
"This day you shall be with me in paradise."
Kind Jesus, show me such mercy at the hour of
    my death. Amen.

6. O blessed Jesus, loving king and kind friend,
be mindful of the sorrows you experienced
when you hung naked on the cross
as all your friends and enemies stood there before
    you.
You found comfort only in your blessed Mother,
the beloved disciple, and Mary Magdalene,
as they stood faithfully at the foot of the cross.
As your death drew near, you commended your
    Mother
to the beloved disciple, saying, *"Woman, here is
    your son."*
Mindful of your bitter passion, and of the sword
    of sorrow
that pierced your Mother's heart,
I implore you, blessed Jesus, to have compassion
on my afflictions of body and spirit
and give me comfort in all my troubles. Amen.

7. O blessed Jesus, source of endless pity,
for love of us, you cried out from the tree of the
   cross,
"*I thirst,*" thirsting for the salvation of our souls.
Mindful of your great longing for us,
extinguish in me the desire of the flesh,
the desire of the eyes, and the pride in riches,
and so moderate and temper all my desires
that they may be according to your holy will.
Amen.

8. O blessed Jesus, our hearts' delight,
I appeal to you by the sour wine and bitter gall
you tasted for me in your passion,
that, at the hour of my death,
I may worthily and devoutly receive
your blessed Body and Blood in the sacrament of
   the altar
as a remedy for my sins and a comfort for my
   soul.
Amen.

9. O blessed Jesus, our strength and our joy,
be mindful of the great anguish and distress
you suffered for me and for all humankind
when, in the midst of your dying
and the scoffing of your enemies,
you cried out to your Father with a mighty voice,
"*My God, my God, why have you forsaken me?*"

By this painful agony of your dear Son,
O holy God,
do not forsake us at the hour of our death.
Amen.

10. O blessed Jesus, our first beginning and our
   last end,
be mindful that you were immersed
from the top of your head to the soles of your
   feet
when you were drowned for us
in the waters of your painful passion.
Mindful of the great pain of your five precious
   wounds,
I, who am immersed in sin, implore you,
blessed Jesus,
to teach me your great commandment of love.
Amen.

11. O blessed Jesus, abyss of endless mercy,
by the depth of the five wounds
that pierced your tender flesh, your sacred heart
and the very marrow of your bones,
be pleased to draw me out of my sins
and hide me forever from your wrath
in the holes of your hands, feet, and side,
as the day of doom approaches. Amen.

12. O blessed mirror of truth,
token of unity, and bond of charity,

be mindful of your innumerable pains and
  wounds
and the precious blood that bathed your entire
  body.
You could never have done more for us
than you did in your clean, virginal body.
Therefore, kind Jesus, in remembrance of your
  passion,
with your precious blood write all your wounds
  in my heart,
so that I may continue to praise and thank you
to the end of my life. Amen.

13. O blessed Jesus, mighty and victorious king,
be mindful of the sorrow you suffered
when all the strength of your body failed you
  completely,
and, inclining your head, you said, *"It is finished."*
In memory of that anguish and sorrow,
blessed Jesus, have mercy on me in my last hour,
and deliver my soul from anguish
and my spirit from trouble.
Amen.

14. O blessed Jesus, only-begotten Son of the
  Father,
and shining likeness of God's very self,
be mindful that on the cross
*you commended your spirit into your Father's
  hands*

and turned over your life to him with a great cry,
a torn body, and a broken heart,
to show us the depths of your mercy.
In memory of that precious death,
I implore you, Lord of the souls in bliss,
strengthen me to withstand the world, the flesh,
    and the devil
that I may be dead to the world and alive to you,
and at my departure from this life
receive my pilgrim soul into glory. Amen.

15. O blessed Jesus, true and noble vine,
be mindful of your passion
and the abundant shedding of your blood,
as if it had been pressed from a ripe cluster of
    grapes.
They pressed your blessed body in the winepress
    of the cross,
and gave us both blood and water
to drink from your pierced body,
until not one drop of water or blood was left in it.
Towards the end of your agony,
you hung high on the cross like a bundle of myrrh
as your tender flesh changed color with the pallor
    of dying
as all the vital fluids in your flesh dried up.
In memory of this bitter passion, sweet Jesus,
wound my sinful heart
and nourish me with the water of repentance
and the tears of love, both night and day.

Good Jesus, turn me wholly to you
and dwell in my heart forever,
so that at my life's end,
I may deserve to praise you forever
with all the saints in glory. Amen.[47]

The Hours of the Passion

Like some other early churches, the Church of Rome observed three times of prayer on a daily basis in memory of the passion and death of Jesus.

Here is the testimony of St. Hippolytus of Rome around a.d. 215:

> *If you are at home at the third hour [9 A.M.], pray and praise God. If you are someplace else at that time, pray to God in your heart, for it was at that hour that Christ was nailed to the tree of the cross.*
>
> *Pray in the same way at the sixth hour [noon], for when Christ was nailed to the wood of the cross, the day was divided in two and darkness fell. Pray a powerful prayer at that time, imitating the voice of him who cried aloud and made all creation dark. . . .*
>
> *At the ninth hour [3 P.M.], prolong your prayer and praise, for at that hour Christ's side was pierced with a lance and poured out water and blood.*

These times of prayer are recommended for all Fridays of the year, and particularly during Lent and Holy Week. The psalms and readings suit the times and sense of Jesus' passion, and the prayers are drawn from a medieval Latin manuscript that preserved this tradition of prayer.

Friday at Midmorning

Let us glory in the cross of our Lord Jesus Christ.
~In him is our salvation, life, and resurrection.

Psalm 7:1–2, 7–11, 17

Jesus Is Nailed to the Cross

Lord, my God, I take refuge in you.
From my pursuers save me and rescue me,
lest they tear me to pieces like a lion
and drag me off with no one to rescue me.

Lord, rise up in your anger,
rise against the fury of my foes;
my God, awake! You will give judgment.
Let the company of nations gather round you,
take your seat above them on high.
The Lord is the judge of the peoples.

Give judgment for me, Lord; I am just
and innocent of heart.
Put an end to the evil of the wicked!
Make the just stand firm,
you who test mind and heart,
O just God!

God is the shield that protects me,
who saves the upright of heart.
God is a just judge,
slow to anger,

but threatening the wicked every day,
all those who will not repent.

I will thank the LORD who is just:
I will sing to the LORD, the Most High.

Glory to the Holy and Undivided Trinity:
now and always and forever and ever. Amen.

READING   **9 A.M.**   **MARK 15:22–28**[48]
The soldiers took Jesus to a place called Golgotha,
which means "The Place of the Skull." There they
tried to give him wine mixed with a drug called
myrrh, but Jesus would not drink it. Then they
crucified him and divided his clothes among
themselves, throwing dice to see who would get
each piece of clothing. It was nine o'clock in the
morning when they crucified him. The notice of
accusation against him said: "The King of the
Jews." They also crucified two bandits with Jesus,
one on his right and the other on his left.

SILENCE

RESPONSE
Do not leave me alone in my distress;
~COME CLOSE, THERE IS NONE ELSE TO HELP.

PRAYER
Let us pray *(pause for quiet prayer)*:
Lord Jesus Christ,
at midmorning Pilate's soldiers
led you to the hill of Golgotha

and nailed you to the cross of pain
for the salvation of the world.
By the grace of your five precious wounds,
forgive us our sins, uproot our sinful tendencies,
and inspire us to walk the way of the cross with
    you,
now and forever.
~Amen.

May our Lord Jesus Christ,
who was torn with scourges,
crowned with a wreath of thorns,
and raised on a cross for us,
✝ bless us and keep us.
~Amen.

Friday at Noon
Let us glory in the cross of our Lord Jesus Christ.
~In him is our salvation, life, and resurrection.

Psalm 17:1–12, 15   Jesus Appeals to God
Lord, hear a cause that is just,
pay heed to my cry.
Turn your ear to my prayer,
no deceit is on my lips.

From you may judgment come forth.
Your eyes discern the truth.

You search my heart, you visit me by night.
You test me and you find in me no wrong.
My words are not sinful like human words.

I am here and I call, you will hear me, O God.
Turn your ear to me; hear my words.
Display your great love, you whose right hand
    saves
your friends from those who rebel against them.

Guard me as the apple of your eye.
Hide me in the shadow of your wings
from the violent attacks of the wicked.

My foes encircle me with deadly intent.
Their hearts tight shut, their mouths speak
    proudly.
They advance against me, and now they surround
    me.

Their eyes are watching to strike me to the ground,
as though they were lions ready to claw
or like some young lion crouched in hiding.

As for me, in my justice I shall see your face
and be filled, when I awake, with the sight of
    your glory.

Glory to the Holy and Undivided Trinity:
now and always and forever and ever. Amen.

READING   12 NOON   MARK 15:29–33[49]
People passing by shook their heads and hurled
insults at Jesus: "Aha! You were going to tear
down the Temple and build it up again in three
days! Now come down from the cross and save
yourself!" In the same way the chief priests and
the teachers of the Law made fun of Jesus, saying

106 The Season of Lent

to one another, "He saved others but he cannot save himself! Let us see the Messiah, the king of Israel, come down from the cross now, and we will believe in him!" And the two who were crucified with Jesus insulted him also. At noon the whole country was covered with darkness, which lasted for three hours.

SILENCE

RESPONSE

These people stare at me and gloat;
~THEY DIVIDE MY CLOTHING AMONG THEM.

PRAYER

Let us pray *(pause for quiet prayer)*:

Lord Jesus Christ,
as you hung on the cross at noon,
the whole country was plunged into darkness.
By the grace of your precious blood,
grant us lasting light for our souls and bodies
and bring us in safety to the unfading glories
of our heavenly home,
where you live and reign forever and ever.
~AMEN.

May our Lord Jesus Christ,
who was taunted by passersby
and abused by criminals
as he hung in darkness on the cross,
✝ bless us and keep us.
~AMEN.

Friday at Midafternoon

Let us glory in the cross of our Lord Jesus Christ.
~In him is our salvation, life, and resurrection.

Psalm 54:1–4, 6–7   **Jesus Pleads for Help**

O God, save me by your name;
by your power uphold my cause.
O God, hear my prayer;
listen to the words of my mouth.

For the proud have risen against me,
ruthless foes seek my life.
They have no regard for God.
But I have God for my help.
The Lord upholds my life.

I will sacrifice to you with willing heart
and praise your name, O Lord, for it is good;
for you have rescued me from all my distress
and my eyes have seen the downfall of my foes.

Glory to the Holy and Undivided Trinity:
now and always and forever and ever. Amen.

Reading   **3 p.m.**   **Mark 15:34, 37–39**[50]

At three o'clock Jesus cried out with a loud shout,
"Eloi, Eloi, lema sabachthani?" which means, "My
God, my God, why did you abandon me?" With a
loud cry Jesus died. The curtain hanging in the
Temple was torn in two, from top to bottom. The
army officer who was standing there in front of
the cross saw how Jesus had died. "This man was
really the Son of God," he said. Some women were

there, looking on from a distance. Among them were Mary Magdalene, Mary the mother of the younger James and of Joseph, and Salome. They had followed Jesus while he was in Galilee and had helped him. Many other women who had come to Jerusalem with him were there also.

SILENCE

RESPONSE

They tear holes in my hands and my feet.
~AND LAY ME IN THE DUST OF DEATH.

PRAYER

Let us pray *(pause for quiet prayer)*:

Lord Jesus Christ,
as you were expiring in agony at midafternoon,
you promised paradise to a repentant criminal,
handed over your spirit to your Father,
and descended among the imprisoned spirits
for their enlightenment.
By the blood and water
that gushed from your pierced side,
wash away all our sins,
renew in us a true and life-giving spirit,
and bring us at last to the resurrection of the body
and life everlasting in the world to come,
where you live and reign with the Father and the
    Holy Spirit,
now and forever.
~AMEN.

May our Lord Jesus Christ,
who breathed his last at midafternoon
in the presence of his mother
and of the other faithful women from Galilee,
† bless us and keep us.
~AMEN.

A Devotion in Honor of
the Mother of Sorrows

In the mid-thirteenth century seven city councilors of
Florence left politics and founded a religious association to venerate Jesus' mother under the title "Our
Lady of Sorrows." By the time the association was officially approved by Pope Benedict XI in 1304, it had
grown into the Order of Servites, devoted to honor and
preach Mary's seven sorrows. In modern times a
novena to the Sorrowful Mother became very popular,
especially in the Servite Church of Chicago, and
emerged as a powerful form of intercession and consolation to thousands of the afflicted and depressed of
our time. As Mother of the Church and of each baptized person in particular, she is one to whom we turn
for protection, for help in time of need, and for consolation in time of trouble and distress. Devotion to Our
Lady of Sorrows is particularly appropriate during
Lent and Holy Week.

In the name of the Father, † and of the Son,
and of the Holy Spirit.
~AMEN.

HYMN   **MOTHER OF US ALL**

Mary crowned with living light,
temple of the Lord,
place of peace and holiness,
shelter of the Word.

Mystery of sinless life
in our fallen race,
free from shadow, you reflect
plenitude of grace.

Virgin-Mother of our God,
lift us when we fall,
who were named upon the cross
Mother of us all.

Father, Son, and Paraclete,
heaven sings your praise,
Mary magnifies your name
through eternal days.[51]

PSALM 149:1–6, 9   **GOD DELIGHTS IN HIS PEOPLE**

ANTIPHON BLEST IS THE VIRGIN MARY
WHO STOOD AT THE CROSS OF JESUS
AND NOW REIGNS WITH HIM FOREVER.

Sing a new song to the LORD,
sing praise in the assembly of the faithful.
Let Israel rejoice in its Maker,
let Zion's people exult in their king.
Let them praise God's name with dancing
and make music with timbrel and harp.

For the LORD takes delight in his people,
and crowns the poor with salvation.
Let the faithful rejoice in their glory,
shout for joy and take their rest.
Let the praise of God be on their lips
and a two-edged sword in their hand,
to deal out the sentence preordained:
this honor is for all God's faithful.

ANTIPHON BLEST IS THE VIRGIN MARY
WHO STOOD AT THE CROSS OF JESUS
AND NOW REIGNS WITH HIM FOREVER.

PSALM PRAYER

Let us pray *(pause for quiet prayer)*:

God of all consolation,
you permitted the sharp sword of separation
to pierce the immaculate heart of Mary.
By her loving intercession
reveal to us the secrets of the blessed passion
of your only Son our Savior,
and bring us at last to the home-haven of heaven;
through the same Christ our Lord.
~AMEN.

READING   TEARS   LAMENTATIONS 1:2, 12

She weeps bitterly in the night, with tears on her
cheeks; among all her lovers she has no one to
comfort her; all her friends have dealt treacher-
ously with her, they have become her enemies. Is

it nothing to you, all you who pass by? Look and see if there is any sorrow like my sorrow, which was brought upon me, which the LORD inflicted on the day of his fierce anger.

SILENCE

RESPONSE

Let us stand by the cross with Mary the Mother of Jesus,

~WHOSE SOUL WAS PIERCED BY A SWORD OF SORROW.

CANTICLE OF THE VIRGIN MARY   LUKE 1:46–55
ANTIPHON IS THIS THE WOMAN THAT WAS CALLED THE PERFECTION OF BEAUTY, THE JOY OF ALL THE EARTH?

My soul † proclaims the greatness of the Lord,
my spirit rejoices in God my Savior,
for you, Lord, have looked with favor on your
    lowly servant.

From this day all generations will call me blessed:
    you, the Almighty, have done great things
        for me
    and holy is your name.
    You have mercy on those who fear you,
    from generation to generation.

You have shown strength with your arm
and scattered the proud in their conceit,
casting down the mighty from their thrones
    and lifting up the lowly.

You have filled the hungry with good things
and sent the rich away empty.

You have come to the aid of your servant Israel,
to remember the promise of mercy,
the promise made to our forebears,
to Abraham and his children forever.

Glory to the Father, and to the Son,
and to the Holy Spirit:
as it was in the beginning, is now,
and will be forever. Amen.

ANTIPHON IS THIS THE WOMAN THAT WAS CALLED
THE PERFECTION OF BEAUTY, THE JOY OF ALL THE
EARTH?

LITANY OF THE BLESSED VIRGIN MARY
(SEE PAGES 221–223 OR 223–225)

CLOSING PRAYER
Jesus, Man of Sorrows and acquainted with grief,
as you were suffering and dying on the cross
your sweet Mother's soul was pierced
by a sword of sorrow and compassion.
By her prayers and tears,
listen to our pleas and help us in our needs.
May we who meditate on her sorrows
enjoy the fruit of your suffering and death
and rise with you in your glorious resurrection.
You live and reign, now and forever.
~AMEN.

May the glorious passion of our Lord Jesus Christ
✝ bring us to the joys of paradise.
~AMEN.

Devotions for Holy Week

The pinnacle of the Church year comes in Holy Week,
the week that stretches between Palm (or Passion)
Sunday and Easter Sunday.

> *In Holy Week, the Church celebrates the myster-*
> *ies of salvation accomplished by Christ in the last*
> *days of his earthly life, beginning with his mes-*
> *sianic entry into Jerusalem. . . . Holy Week begins*
> *with Palm Sunday, which unites the royal splen-*
> *dor of Christ with the proclamation of his passion.*
> *The procession, commemorating Christ's mes-*
> *sianic entry into Jerusalem, is joyous and popu-*
> *lar in character. The faithful usually keep palm or*
> *olive branches, or other greenery which have*
> *been blessed on Palm Sunday in their homes or*
> *in their workplaces. [They] are kept in the home*
> *as a witness to faith in Jesus Christ, the mes-*
> *sianic king, and his paschal victory.*[52]

Meal Prayers for Holy Week

BEFORE AND AFTER DINNER

LEADER: Christ Jesus emptied himself,

ALL: ~TAKING THE FORM OF A SLAVE,
BEING BORN IN HUMAN LIKENESS.
AND BEING FOUND IN HUMAN FORM, HE HUMBLED
    HIMSELF
AND BECAME OBEDIENT TO THE POINT OF DEATH—
EVEN DEATH ON A CROSS.

Leader: Holy, mighty, and immortal God,
look on this family of yours,
for which our Lord Jesus Christ
did not hesitate to surrender himself to the wicked
and to undergo the torment of the cross.

All: ~Amen.

Leader: Our Father . . . *(Continue in unison.)*

A Devotion to the Blessed Passion

The sections of the four Gospels that recount the sufferings and death of Jesus are distributed over the
liturgies of Holy Week but are also appropriate reading and meditation for private prayer to deepen our
appreciation of the paschal mystery: Mark 14–15;
Matthew 26–27; Luke 22–23; John 18–19. They may
also be read in brief selections during the following
devotion to the Passion.

In the name of the Father, † and of the Son,
and of the Holy Spirit.

~Amen.

Hymn for Holy Week

You make your way alone: a victim, Lord,
whose sacrifice will see death overthrown.
What can we say, so wretched, overawed,
when all the pain you bear should be our own?

The sins are ours, and ours should be the blame;
why should you suffer in the sinner's place?
Lord, break our hearts, and make us feel your
     shame,

for only such compassion shares your grace.

We see the anguish of the grievous night:
the evening came with weeping, which will last
until the third day breaks, and new delight
comes surging with you, Lord, when grief has
    passed.

So fill us with compassion: those who share
your sorrow now, will share your glory, too,
and end earth's days of darkness and despair
in Easter laughter, wild with joy for you.[53]

PSALM 22   THE SUFFERING SERVANT OF GOD

ANTIPHON THE SON OF MAN IS GOING TO BE BETRAYED
INTO HUMAN HANDS, AND THEY WILL KILL HIM, AND ON
THE THIRD DAY HE WILL BE RAISED.

My God, my God, why have you forsaken me?
You are far from my plea and the cry of my
    distress.
O my God, I call by day and you give me no reply;
I call by night and I find no peace.

Yet you, O God, are holy,
enthroned on the praises of Israel.
In you our forebears put their trust;
they trusted and you set them free.
When they cried to you, they escaped.
In you they trusted and never in vain.

But I am a worm and no man,
the butt of all, the laughingstock of the people.

All who see me deride me.
They curl their lips, they toss their heads.
"He trusted in the Lord, let him save him,
and release him if this is his friend."

Yes, it was you who took me from the womb,
entrusted me to my mother's breast.
To you I was committed from my birth,
from my mother's womb you have been my God.
Do not leave me alone in my distress.
Come close, there is none else to help.

Many bulls have surrounded me,
fierce bulls of Bashan close me in.
Against me they open wide their jaws,
like lions, rending and roaring.

Like water I am poured out,
disjointed are all my bones.
My heart has become like wax,
it is melted within my breast.
Parched as burnt clay is my throat,
my tongue cleaves to my jaws.

Many dogs have surrounded me,
a band of the wicked beset me.
They tear holes in my hands and my feet
and lay me in the dust of death.

I can count every one of my bones.
These people stare at me and gloat;
they divide my clothing among them.
They cast lots for my robe.

O Lord, do not leave me alone,
my strength, make haste to help me!
Rescue my soul from the sword,
my life from the grip of these dogs.
Save my life from the jaws of these lions,
my soul from the horns of these oxen.

Antiphon The Son of Man is going to be betrayed
into human hands, and they will kill him, and on
the third day he will be raised.

Psalm Prayer

Let us pray *(pause for quiet prayer):*

Lord Jesus Christ, Man of Sorrows,
you came to do the will of the One who sent you:
betrayed by the kiss of Judas,
condemned to death by Pontius Pilate,
mocked, flogged, and crowned with thorns,
pierced with nails, scorned by unbelievers,
you were laid in the dust of death.
By your holy and glorious wounds,
soften our hard hearts,
teach us true repentance for our sins,
and bring us to the victory you have won for us,
O Savior of the world,
living and reigning, now and forever.
~Amen.

Reading   The Hour   John 12:23–26

The hour has come for the Son of Man to be

glorified. Very truly, I tell you, unless a grain of wheat falls into the earth, it remains just a single grain; but if it dies, it bears much fruit. Those who love their life lose it, and those who hate their life in this world will keep it for eternal life. Whoever serves me must follow me, and where I am, there will my servant be also. Whoever serves me, the Father will honor.

SILENCE

RESPONSE

They tear holes in my hands and my feet
~AND LAY ME IN THE DUST OF DEATH.

CANTICLE OF THE PROPHET ISAIAH (53:1–5)

ANTIPHON PILATE WROTE A NOTICE AND PUT IT ON THE CROSS: "JESUS OF NAZARETH, THE KING OF THE JEWS."

Who would have believed what we have heard
and to whom has the power of the LORD been
    revealed?

He grew up before the LORD like a tender plant,
like a root out of arid ground.
He has no beauty, no majesty to draw our eyes,
no grace to make us delight in him.

He was despised and rejected,
a man of sorrows and acquainted with grief.
Like one from whom people hid their faces
he was despised and we esteemed him not.

Surely he has borne our grief and carried our
    sorrows;
yet we considered him stricken,
smitten by God, and afflicted.
He was wounded for our transgressions,
he was bruised for our iniquities.
The punishment that brought us peace was laid
    upon him,
and by his wounds we are healed.

To the One seated on the throne and to the Lamb
be blessing and honor and glory and might
forever and ever!

ANTIPHON PILATE WROTE A NOTICE AND PUT IT ON
THE CROSS: "JESUS OF NAZARETH, THE KING OF THE
JEWS."

A LITANY OF THE SACRED PASSION
Lord Jesus, at the Last Supper you knew that Judas,
    one of the Twelve, would betray you:
~GOOD LORD, DELIVER US FROM TREACHERY.

Lord Jesus, during the supper, you humbly
    washed the feet of your disciples:
~GOOD LORD, MAKE US MEEK AND HUMBLE OF HEART.

Lord Jesus, at the Last Supper, you gave us the
    sacrament of your broken body and outpoured
    blood:
~GOOD LORD, WE WORSHIP THE SEAL OF THE NEW
AND ETERNAL COVENANT.

Lord Jesus, you asked your disciples to watch and
pray with you in the Garden of Gethsemane:
~GOOD LORD, KEEP US AWAKE AND WATCHFUL.

Lord Jesus, at your arrest your friends fled in fear
and deserted you:
~GOOD LORD, GIVE US COURAGE IN TIME OF TRIAL.

Lord Jesus, you were falsely accused and
condemned for speaking the truth:
~GOOD LORD, MAY WE SPEAK TRUTH IN THE FACE
OF INJUSTICE.

Lord Jesus, in the courtyard of the high priest,
Simon Peter swore that he did not know you:
~GOOD LORD, MAKE US FAITHFUL IN TIME
OF TEMPTATION.

Lord Jesus, Pilate traded you for a murderer
and handed you over to crucifixion:
~GOOD LORD, HAVE MERCY ON US SINNERS.

Lord Jesus, you were mocked, insulted, and beaten
by Pilate's soldiers:
~GOOD LORD, MAY WE SUFFER GLADLY FOR YOUR SAKE.

Lord Jesus, on the cross you were taunted and
derided as King of the Jews:
~GOOD LORD, MAY WE ALWAYS LIVE IN OBEDIENCE
TO YOU.

Lord Jesus, you cried out in agony to your Father
    and died with a loud cry:
~GOOD LORD, HAVE MERCY ON US, NOW AND AT
THE HOUR OF OUR DEATH.

Lord Jesus, the Roman centurion recognized you
    as the Son of God:
~GOOD LORD, MAY WE ALWAYS PRAISE AND EXALT YOU
AS OUR BLESSED SAVIOR.

(Pause for special intentions.)

We adore you, O Christ, and we bless you,
~FOR BY YOUR HOLY CROSS YOU HAVE REDEEMED
THE WORLD.

THE LORD'S PRAYER

CLOSING PRAYER
Lord Jesus Christ,
you were fastened with nails to the wood
    of the cross
and raised on high for all to see.
As the sun grew dark and the earth quaked,
you surrendered your spirit to your Father,
descended among the dead,
broke open the gates of hell,
and freed those bound in darkness.
As angel choirs rejoiced,
you were raised to life again on the third day,
destroying death by your own death

and canceling the power of sin.
By these mighty deeds on our behalf,
rescue us from our blindness and tepidity,
inspire us anew by your Holy Spirit,
and lead us into a life of prayer and service
worthy of your awesome sacrifice,
O Savior of the world,
living and reigning, now and forever.
~Amen.

May the glorious passion of our Lord Jesus Christ
† bring us to the joys of paradise.
~Amen.

Devotions for the Easter Triduum

The sacred Triduum extends from the Mass of the
Lord's Supper on Holy Thursday evening through the
Vespers of Easter Sunday. It is the very center of
the church's year of grace and makes present for us
sacramentally the high mysteries of the passion,
death, and resurrection of the Lord Jesus. These forms
of prayer supplement and enhance the Lord's Supper,
the Liturgy of Good Friday, and the baptismal vigil of
Easter. As St. Bonaventure reminds us: "How whole-
some it is, always to meditate on the cross of Christ."[54]

*It is far sweeter to see you born into the world of
the Virgin Mother than to see you born in splendor of the Father before the morning star; to see
you die on the cross, than to see you ruling the*

*angels in heaven. Nowhere do I perceive Christ
more truly than where he hangs on the cross.*

St. Anselm of Canterbury (1033–1109) [55]

In the name of the Father, ✝ and of the Son,
and of the Holy Spirit.
~AMEN.

Pilate had Jesus whipped,
~AND HANDED HIM OVER TO BE CRUCIFIED.

Pilate wrote a notice and put it on the cross:
~"JESUS OF NAZARETH, THE KING OF THE JEWS."

All you who pass by, look and see:
~IS THERE ANY SORROW LIKE THE SORROW THAT
AFFLICTS ME?

Jesus said: "Forgive them, Father!
~THEY DON'T KNOW WHAT THEY ARE DOING."

PSALM 86:1–10, 12–13   JESUS ASKS TO BE RESCUED

ANTIPHON THEY WILL MOCK HIM AND SCOURGE HIM
AND SPIT ON HIM, AND PUT HIM TO DEATH.

Turn your ear, O LORD, and give answer
for I am poor and needy.
Preserve my life, for I am faithful;
save the servant who trusts in you.

You are my God, have mercy on me, Lord,
for I cry to you all the day long.

Give joy to your servant, O Lord,
for to you I lift up my soul.

O Lord, you are good and forgiving,
full of love to all who call.
Give heed, O LORD, to my prayer
and attend to the sound of my voice.

In the day of distress I will call
and surely you will reply.
Among the gods there is none like you, O Lord,
nor work to compare with yours.

All the nations shall come to adore you
and glorify your name, O Lord,
for you are great and do marvelous deeds,
you who alone are God.

I will praise you, Lord my God, with all my heart
and glorify your name forever;
for your love to me has been great,
you have saved me from the depths of the grave.

ANTIPHON THEY WILL MOCK HIM AND SCOURGE HIM
AND SPIT ON HIM, AND PUT HIM TO DEATH.

PSALM PRAYER

Let us pray *(pause for quiet prayer):*

Abba, dear Father,
look upon this family of yours
for which our Lord Jesus Christ
willingly endured the torment of the cross
at the hands of the wicked.

He lives and reigns with you and the Holy Spirit,
now and forever.

~Amen.

Reading　　Holy Thursday　　Luke 18:31–34[56]

Jesus took the twelve disciples aside and said to
them, "Listen! We are going to Jerusalem where
everything the prophets wrote about the Son of
Man will come true. He will be handed over to
the Gentiles, who will make fun of him, insult
him, and spit on him. They will whip him and
kill him, but three days later he will rise to life."
But the disciples did not understand any of these
things; the meaning of the words was hidden
from them, and they did not know what Jesus was
talking about.

Silence

Response

We adore you, O Christ, and we bless you,

~For by your holy cross you have redeemed
the world.

Reading　　Good Friday　　Romans 5:6–10[57]

When we were still helpless, Christ died for the
wicked at the time that God chose. It is a difficult
thing for someone to die for a righteous person. It
may even be that someone might dare to die for a
good person. But God has shown us how much he
loves us—it was while we were still sinners that

Christ died for us! By his blood we are now put right with God; how much more, then, will we be saved by him from God's anger! We were God's enemies, but he made us his friends through the death of his Son. Now that we are God's friends, how much more will we be saved by Christ's life!

SILENCE

RESPONSE
Christ will cover you with the wings of his cross.
~YOU WILL BE SAFE UNDER HIS CARE.

READING **HOLY SATURDAY** **JOB 19:25, 26B–27**
I know that my Redeemer lives, and that at the last he will stand upon the earth. Then in my flesh I shall see God, whom I shall see on my side, and my eyes shall behold, and not another. My heart faints within me!

SILENCE

RESPONSE
We adore you, O Christ, and we bless you,
~FOR BY YOUR HOLY CROSS YOU HAVE REDEEMED THE WORLD.

**CANTICLE OF ST. PETER
THE APOSTLE** **1 PETER 2:21–25** [58]
ANTIPHON JESUS WAS PIERCED FOR OUR OFFENSES, CRUSHED FOR OUR SINS.

Christ himself suffered for you
and left you an example,
so that you would follow
in his steps.
He committed no sin,
and no one ever heard a lie
come from his lips.

When he was insulted,
he did not answer back with an insult;
when he suffered,
he did not threaten,
but placed his hopes in God,
the righteous Judge.

Christ himself carried our sins
in his body to the cross,
so that we might die to sin
and live for righteousness.
It is by his wounds
that you have been healed.

You were like sheep
that had lost their way,
but now you have been brought back
to follow the Shepherd and Keeper of your souls.

Glory to the Father, and to the Son,
    and to the Holy Spirit:

as it was in the beginning, is now,
    and will be forever. Amen.

ANTIPHON JESUS WAS PIERCED FOR OUR OFFENSES, CRUSHED FOR OUR SINS.

LITANY OF THE PASSION

Lord Jesus, betrayed by the kiss of Judas
   in the Garden of Gethsemane:
~HEAR US AND HAVE MERCY.

Lord Jesus, condemned to death in the court
   of Pontius Pilate:
~HEAR US AND HAVE MERCY.

Lord Jesus, flogged for us at the pillar:
~HEAR US AND HAVE MERCY.

Lord Jesus, crowned with a wreath of thorns for us:
~HEAR US AND HAVE MERCY.

Lord Jesus, carrying the cross to Golgotha for us:
~HEAR US AND HAVE MERCY.

Lord Jesus, nailed to the cross for us:
~HEAR US AND HAVE MERCY.

Lord Jesus, mocked, derided, and insulted
   on the cross:
~HEAR US AND HAVE MERCY.

Lord Jesus, dead on the cross of pain for us:
~HEAR US AND HAVE MERCY.

Lord Jesus, buried for us in Joseph's tomb:
~HEAR US AND HAVE MERCY.

Lord Jesus, raised from the dead on the third day:
~HEAR US AND HAVE MERCY.

Lord Jesus, flooding the world with your Holy
    Spirit:
~HEAR US AND HAVE MERCY.

(Pause for special intentions.)

CLOSING PRAYER
Lord Jesus, suffering servant of God,
for our sake and for our salvation,
you were unjustly condemned to death,
mocked, scourged and crowned with thorns,
pierced with nails and scorned by unbelievers.
By your holy and glorious wounds,
shelter us under the shadow of your cross
while we await in sure and certain hope
for your victory over sin and death and hell.
You live and reign forever and ever.
~AMEN.

By his holy and glorious wounds,
may Christ our Lord † protect us and keep us.
~AMEN.

Holy Thursday Devotions
Popular piety is particularly sensitive to the ado-
ration of the Most Blessed Sacrament in the wake
of the Mass of the Lord's Supper. . . . It is an invi-
tation to silent and prolonged adoration of the
wondrous sacrament instituted by Jesus on this

day. . . . After midnight on Holy Thursday, the adoration should conclude without solemnity, since the day of the Lord's passion has already begun.[59]

During the period of adoration, we may use the Devotions to the Sacred Heart of Jesus and to the Blessed Sacrament for Corpus Christi (pages 200–211), the above devotions to the Passion, and the Litanies of the Sacred Heart, the Precious Blood, and the Blessed Sacrament (pages 214–220).

Good Friday Devotions

The Church celebrates the redemptive death of Christ on Good Friday. The Church meditates on the Lord's passion in the afternoon liturgical action, in which she prays for the salvation of the world, adores the cross, and commemorates her very origin in the sacred wound in Christ's side (see John 19:34).[60]

THE WAY OF THE CROSS

This devotion to the Passion, also known as the stations of the cross, is often publicly observed on Good Friday evening, sometime after the solemn liturgy of the day, and is at times accompanied or followed by the singing of the *Stabat Mater* (see below) to memorialize Mary's association with the sorrows of her Son. For those who prefer to perform the stations privately, at home or in church, see "A Biblical Way of the Cross," pages 251–269.

THE *STABAT MATER DOLOROSA*

This poignant hymn describes the sorrows of Our Lady of Compassion as she kept vigil at the foot of the cross.

It is attributed to the thirteenth-century Franciscan
Jacapone da Todi (c. 1230–1306), who composed some
one hundred praise poems on spiritual themes and was
the most famous vernacular poet in Italy before Dante.
This popular hymn became part of the Roman liturgy in
the late Middle Ages and is used on the Feast of Our
Lady of Sorrows (September 15) and, often, during or
after the public celebrations of the way of the cross.

By the cross her vigil keeping,
stood the mournful mother weeping,
where he hung, the dying Lord:
There she waited in her anguish,
seeing Christ in torment languish,
in her heart the piercing sword.

With what pain and desolation,
with what grief and resignation,
Mary watched her dying Son.
Deep the woe of her affliction,
when she saw the crucifixion
of the sole-begotten One.

Him she saw for our salvation
mocked with cruel acclamation,
scourged, and crowned with thorns entwined;
saw him then from judgment taken,
and in death by all forsaken,
till his spirit he resigned.

Who, on Christ's dear mother gazing,
pierced by anguish so amazing,
born of woman, would not weep?

Who, on Christ's dear mother thinking,
such a cup of sorrow drinking,
would not share her sorrows deep? [61]

Holy Saturday Devotions

On Holy Saturday, the Church pauses at the Lord's tomb, meditating on his passion and death, his descent to the dead, and, with prayer and fasting, awaits his resurrection. [62]

The Litanies of the Sacred Heart and of the Precious Blood are appropriate on Holy Saturday (see pages 214–218).

THE FIVE SORROWS OF THE VIRGIN

In some places there exists a Marian devotion *(Maria desolata)* that commemorates Mary "as she waits near the Lord's tomb, an icon of the Virgin Church keeping vigil at the tomb of her Spouse while awaiting the celebration of his resurrection." [63] Here are prayers for that devotion.

1. Gracious Lady, God's mother, for the sorrow that you had when Simeon said that the sword of sorrow would pass through your heart, implore your dear Son that I may have forgiveness for my sinful life, and that I may be received with his blessed children into endless bliss. And good Jesus, for your mother's love and this first sorrow, comfort us in all our needs, bodily and spiritual, and especially for those who pray for me and trust in my prayers.

2. Blessed Mother of God, for that grievous sorrow which you had when you had lost your Son, seeking hastily, weeping and mourning, pray to him our Lord, that I may have the grace to seek for him with tears of love and penitence, and that I may grow in love and come to perfect charity. And good Jesus, God's Son, for your mother's love and for this her second sorrow, comfort us all in our need, bodily and spiritual, and especially those who pray for me and trust in my prayers for them.

3. Blessed Lady, Mother of God, for that dreadful sorrow, when in your soul you saw how your Son was arrested by the wicked, deliver me from every kind of fear of bodily and spiritual enemies, that by grace I may live and die pleasingly to him. And good Jesus, for that dreadful arrest and for the third sorrow of your mother, comfort us in all our need, bodily and spiritual, and especially those who pray for me and trust in my prayers for them.

4. Blessed Lady, at the passion of your Son, for that great sorrow which you suffered in all his pains and his lamentable death, ask grace for me to love that Lord so fervently that through the heat of burning love I may always keep in mind his passion, for the health of my soul and the overthrow of the devil. And good Jesus,

God's Son, for your mother's love and for this her fourth sorrow, comfort us in all our needs, bodily and spiritual, and especially those who pray for me and trust in my prayers for them.

5. Sorrowful Lady, standing mourning in the sight of your dear Son, for the great pain that you had to look on that good Lord and all his bloody wounds, by your power obtain for me both grace and mercy, and accept me into your keeping, and govern me in body and soul, to the honor of your dear Son and for my salvation. And good Jesus, God's Son, for your mother's love and for this her fifth sorrow, comfort us in all our need, bodily and spiritual, and especially those who pray for me and trust in my prayers.[64]

The Fifty Days of Easter

The fifty days of Easter (or Eastertide) constitute the high holy season of the Christian year of grace. It centers upon the now-glorious cross, transfigured by the risen Christ, and on the several Gospel accounts of how the disciples of Jesus experienced the risen Lord. Towards the end of this season we concentrate on Jesus' return to the Father and on Pentecost, the fiftieth and final day of Eastertide, the coming of the Holy Spirit on the infant church at Jerusalem.

In many parishes eggs, the symbol of life, and other Easter foods are blessed after the Vigil or on Sunday morning and then eaten at the Easter dinner.

All through Eastertide the family's baptismal candles may be lit on the family altar or dinner table. After grace is recited at the main meal, Easter water may be sprinkled on all present.

Meal Prayers for Eastertide

Before Dinner

LEADER: We adore your cross, O Lord, alleluia!

ALL: ~AND WE PRAISE AND GLORIFY YOUR HOLY RESURRECTION, ALLELUIA!

LEADER: For by the wood of the cross, alleluia!

ALL: ~JOY CAME INTO THE WHOLE WORLD, ALLELUIA!

LEADER: Creator and Savior of the human race,
worthy of all praise and thanksgiving,
you have established us
on the rock of faith in your risen Son.
Free us from our enemies, seen and unseen,
unite us in the bond of peace,
and save all the oppressed of the earth.
We ask this through Christ our Lord.

ALL: ~AMEN.

LEADER: Lord, have mercy.

ALL: ~CHRIST, HAVE MERCY. LORD, HAVE MERCY.

LEADER: Our Father . . . *(Continue in unison.)*

LEADER: Bless ✝ us, O Lord, and these your gifts
which we are about to receive from your bounty;
through Christ our Lord.

ALL: ~AMEN.

LEADER: May the King of eternal glory
make us sit at his welcome table in heaven.

ALL: ~AMEN.

After Dinner

LEADER: Christ is risen, alleluia!

ALL: ~HE IS RISEN INDEED, ALLELUIA!

O praise the LORD, all you nations,
acclaim God, all you peoples!

Strong is God's love for us;
the LORD is faithful forever.

Glory to the Father, and to the Son,
and to the Holy Spirit:

as it was in the beginning, is now,
and will be forever. Amen.

LEADER: Almighty and most merciful Father,
hear your people who glorify
the resurrection of your Son, our Lord.
Guide them on from this great festival
to eternal gladness,
and from the joy of this solemnity
to the joys that have no end.
We ask this through the same Christ our Lord.
ALL: ~AMEN.

LEADER: Almighty God,
we give you thanks for these and for all your gifts.
You live and reign, now and forever.
ALL: ~AMEN.

LEADER: Reward with eternal life, O Lord,
all those who do us good for your name's sake.
ALL: ~AMEN.

LEADER: May the souls of the faithful departed
through the mercy of God rest in peace.
ALL: ~AMEN.

The *Regina Coeli*

During the Fifty Days of Easter, this twelfth-century Marian anthem replaces the triple Angelus each day.

Rejoice, O Queen of Heaven, alleluia!
~FOR THE SON YOU BORE, ALLELUIA!
HAS ARISEN AS HE PROMISED, ALLELUIA!
PRAY FOR US TO GOD THE FATHER, ALLELUIA!

Rejoice and be glad, O Virgin, Mary, alleluia!
~FOR THE LORD HAS TRULY RISEN, ALLELUIA!

Let us pray:

Living and deathless God,
you have given joy to the world
by the resurrection of your Son, our Lord Jesus
    Christ.
Through the prayers of his mother, the Virgin
    Mary,
bring us to the happiness of eternal life;
through the same Christ our Lord.
~AMEN.[65]

Daily Devotions during Eastertide
For Use on the Sundays of Eastertide

Christ is risen, alleluia, alleluia!
~HE IS RISEN INDEED, ALLELUIA, ALLELUIA!

A HYMN   **THE RISEN SAVIOR**

Truly, he comes to us: darkness is ended;
now night is over, his light is ascended:

ultimate sunrise, that floods all creation,
bringing his secret from death's desolation.

Night has made way for the great proclamation,
morning has broken, with songs of elation;
Christ comes in light from the depths of his prison,
Death is abandoned and Jesus is risen.

Stripped of the grave-clothes, the body now
 glorious,
rises immortal, forever victorious;
comes to fulfill all the prophets have spoken;
promise of life that will never be broken.

Weeping is over, and death is defeated,
life is recovered and joy is completed;
guards, at the sepulchre, scatter before him.
Jesus is risen, and angels adore him.

Highest, Most Holy, once lost and forsaken:
now, from the sleep of the dead you awaken;
angels appear at the tomb with the story:
"He is not here, but is risen in glory."

Give God the glory and glad adoration,
from whom and *through* whom and *in* whom,
 creation
looks for the joy which, in Christ, we inherit;
praising the Father, the Son, and the Spirit! Amen.[66]

PSALM 47   RESURRECTION AND ASCENSION
ANTIPHON GOD GOES UP WITH SHOUTS OF JOY,
ALLELUIA!

All peoples clap your hands,
cry to God with shouts of joy!
For the LORD, the Most High, we must fear,
great king over all the earth.

~GOD GOES UP WITH SHOUTS OF JOY, ALLELUIA!

God subdues peoples under us
and nations under our feet.
Our inheritance, our glory, is from God,
given to Jacob out of love.

~GOD GOES UP WITH SHOUTS OF JOY, ALLELUIA!

God goes up with shouts of joy;
the LORD goes up with trumpet blast.
Sing praise for God, sing praise,
sing praise to our king, sing praise.

~GOD GOES UP WITH SHOUTS OF JOY, ALLELUIA!

God is king of all the earth,
sing praise with all your skill.
God is king over the nations;
God reigns enthroned in holiness.

~GOD GOES UP WITH SHOUTS OF JOY, ALLELUIA!

The leaders of the people are assembled
with the people of Abraham's God.
The rulers of the earth belong to God,
to God who reigns over all.

~GOD GOES UP WITH SHOUTS OF JOY, ALLELUIA!

Glory to the Father, and to the Son, and to the
    Holy Spirit:

~G<small>OD GOES UP WITH SHOUTS OF JOY,</small> A<small>LLELUIA</small>!

as it was in the beginning, is now, and will be
    forever. Amen.

~G<small>OD GOES UP WITH SHOUTS OF JOY,</small> A<small>LLELUIA</small>!

Psalm Prayer

Let us pray *(Pause for quiet prayer.)*:

Most High God,
you raised your dear Son from the grave
and brought him to sit at your right hand
in the heavenly realm.
By the power of his cross of glory,
lift up our hearts to you
and bring us into everlasting bliss;
through the same Christ Jesus our Lord.
~A<small>MEN</small>.

Reading   The Empty Tomb   Matthew 28:1–6, 8–10

After the Sabbath, as the first day of the week was
dawning, Mary Magdalene and the other Mary
went to see the tomb. And suddenly there was a
great earthquake; for an angel of the Lord, descend-
ing from heaven, came and rolled back the stone
and sat on it. His appearance was like lightning,
and his clothing white as snow. For fear of him the
guards shook and became like dead men. But the
angel said to the women, "Do not be afraid; I know
that you are looking for Jesus who was crucified.

The Fifty Days of Easter **143**

He is not here; for he has been raised, as he said. Come, see the place where he lay." So they left the tomb quickly with fear and great joy, and ran to tell his disciples. Suddenly Jesus met them and said, "Greetings!" And they came to him, took hold of his feet, and worshiped him. Then Jesus said to them, "Do not be afraid; go and tell my brothers to go to Galilee; there they will see me.

(Pause for meditation.)

RESPONSE
Think of yourselves as dead to sin, alleluia!
~BUT ALIVE TO GOD IN CHRIST JESUS, ALLELUIA!

The Song of the Church (Te Deum)[67]
A. We praise you, O God,
we acclaim you as Lord;
all creation worships you,
the Father everlasting.

To you all angels, all the powers of heaven,
the cherubim and seraphim, sing in endless praise:
Holy, holy, holy Lord, God of power and
might,
heaven and earth are full of your glory.

The glorious company of apostles praise you.
The noble fellowship of prophets praise you.
The white-robed army of martyrs praise you.

Throughout the world the holy Church
acclaims you:
Father, of majesty unbounded,
your true and only Son, worthy of all praise,
and the Holy Spirit, advocate and guide.

B. You, Christ, are the king of glory,
the eternal Son of the Father.
When you took our flesh to set us free
you humbly chose the Virgin's womb.

You overcame the sting of death
and opened the kingdom of heaven to all believers.
You are seated at God's right hand in glory.
We believe that you will come to be our judge.

Come then, Lord, and help your people,
bought with the price of your own blood,
and bring us with your saints
to glory everlasting.

C. Save your people, Lord, and bless your
inheritance.
~Govern and uphold them now and always.

Day by day we bless you.
~We praise your name forever.

Keep us today, Lord, from all sin.
~Have mercy on us, Lord, have mercy.

Lord, show us your love and mercy.
~For we have put our trust in you.

In you, Lord, is our hope.
~LET US NEVER BE PUT TO SHAME.

(Pause for prayers of intercession.)

THE LORD'S PRAYER

CLOSING PRAYER
Heavenly Father,
when Christ our Paschal Lamb
shed his blood on the cross
you delivered us from the destroying angel
who passed by our sins for your love.
You led us into the promised land
by a pillar of cloud by day and a pillar of fire
    by night.
Be our rescuing and victorious God again
    each day
as all creation dances and sings:
Christ has risen from the dead!
~AMEN.

Let us bless the Lord, alleluia, alleluia!
~THANKS BE TO GOD, ALLELUIA, ALLELUIA!

May our radiant and dazzling Christ
† lead us from earth to heaven,
from death to life.
~AMEN.

For Use on the Mondays, Wednesdays, and Fridays of Eastertide

Christ has risen from the tomb, alleluia, alleluia!
~WHO FOR OUR SAKE HUNG ON THE CROSS, ALLELUIA, ALLELUIA!

AN EASTER HYMN

That Easter day with joy was bright;
the sun shone out with fairer light,
when, to their longing eyes restored,
the apostles saw their risen Lord.
Alleluia!

O Jesus, King of gentleness,
with constant love our hearts possess;
to you our lips will ever raise
the tribute of our grateful praise.
Alleluia!

O Christ, you are the Lord of all
in this our Easter festival,
for you will be our strength and shield
from every weapon death can wield.
Alleluia!

All praise, O risen Lord, we give
to you, once dead, but now alive!
To God the Father equal praise,
and God the Holy Ghost, we raise!
Alleluia![68]

ANTIPHON CHRIST HAS RISEN FROM THE DEAD,
CONQUERING DEATH BY HIS DEATH,
AND GIVING LIFE TO THOSE IN THE GRAVE!

Let God arise, let the foes be scattered.
Let those who hate God take to flight.
As smoke is blown away so will they be blown away;
like wax that melts before the fire,
so the wicked will perish at the presence of God.

~CHRIST HAS RISEN FROM THE DEAD, CONQUERING
   DEATH BY HIS DEATH,
AND GIVING LIFE TO THOSE IN THE GRAVE!

But the just shall rejoice at the presence of God,
they shall exult and dance for joy.
O sing to the Lord, make music to God's name;
make a highway for the One who rides on the
   clouds.
Rejoice in the LORD, exult before God.

~CHRIST HAS RISEN FROM THE DEAD, CONQUERING
   DEATH BY HIS DEATH,
AND GIVING LIFE TO THOSE IN THE GRAVE!

You have gone up on high; you have taken captives,
receiving people in tribute, O God,
even those who rebel, into your dwelling, O LORD.

~CHRIST HAS RISEN FROM THE DEAD, CONQUERING
   DEATH BY HIS DEATH,
AND GIVING LIFE TO THOSE IN THE GRAVE!

May the Lord be blessed day after day.
God our savior bears our burdens;
this God of ours is a God who saves.
The LORD our God holds the keys of death.

~CHRIST HAS RISEN FROM THE DEAD, CONQUERING
   DEATH BY HIS DEATH,
AND GIVING LIFE TO THOSE IN THE GRAVE!

The stone which the builders rejected
has become the cornerstone.
This is the work of the LORD,
a marvel in our eyes.
This day was made by the LORD;
we rejoice and are glad.

~CHRIST HAS RISEN FROM THE DEAD, CONQUERING
   DEATH BY HIS DEATH,
AND GIVING LIFE TO THOSE IN THE GRAVE!

Glory to the Father, and to the Son, and to the
   Holy Spirit:

~CHRIST HAS RISEN FROM THE DEAD, CONQUERING
   DEATH BY HIS DEATH,
AND GIVING LIFE TO THOSE IN THE GRAVE!

as it was in the beginning, is now, and will be
   forever. Amen.

~CHRIST HAS RISEN FROM THE DEAD, CONQUERING
   DEATH BY HIS DEATH,
AND GIVING LIFE TO THOSE IN THE GRAVE!

PSALM PRAYER

Let us pray *(pause for quiet prayer)*:

Holy, mighty, and deathless God,
on the third day after his crucifixion,
you raised your dear Son from the grave,
vindicated him in the eyes of his disciples,
and glorified him before the minions of hell.
By his glorious resurrection,
bring us from death to life and from earth
    to heaven
as we sing aloud the hymn of victory.
We ask this through Jesus our risen Savior,
who lives and reigns with you and the life-giving
    Spirit,
now and always and forever and ever.
~AMEN.

THE SPICE-BEARING

READING   **WOMEN**   **MARK 16:1–2, 5–7**

When the Sabbath was over, Mary Magdalene, and
Mary the mother of James, and Salome bought
spices so that they might go and anoint him. And
very early on the first day of the week, when the
sun had risen, they went to the tomb. As they
entered the tomb, they saw a young man, dressed in
a white robe, sitting on the right side; and they
were alarmed. But he said to them, "Do not be
alarmed; you are looking for Jesus of Nazareth, who
was crucified. He has been raised; he is not here.

Look, there is the place they laid him. But go, and tell his disciples and Peter that he is going ahead of you to Galilee; there you will see him just as he told you.

(Pause for meditation.)

RESPONSE
Christ has been raised from the dead, alleluia!
~AND WILL NEVER DIE AGAIN, ALLELUIA!

1 CORINTHIANS 5:7–8;
ROMANS 6:9–11;
EASTER ANTHEM   1 CORINTHIANS 15:20–22

ANTIPHON WE ADORE YOUR CROSS, O LORD, AND WE PRAISE AND GLORIFY YOUR HOLY RESURRECTION; BY THE WOOD OF THE CROSS, JOY CAME INTO THE WHOLE WORLD.

Our Paschal Lamb, Christ, has been sacrificed.
Therefore let us celebrate the festival,
Not with the old yeast, the yeast of malice and evil,
But with the unleavened bread of sincerity
    and truth, alleluia!

~BY THE WOOD OF THE CROSS, JOY CAME INTO THE WHOLE WORLD.

Christ, being raised from the dead, will never
    die again;
Death no longer has dominion over him.
The death he died he died to sin, once for all;
But the life he lives, he lives to God.

So you also must consider yourselves dead to sin,
And alive to God in Christ Jesus our Lord, alleluia!

~BY THE WOOD OF THE CROSS, JOY CAME INTO THE
WHOLE WORLD.

Christ has been raised from the dead,
The first-fruits of those who have died.
For since death came through a human being,
the resurrection of the dead has also come
    through a human being.
For as all die in Adam,
So all will be made alive in Christ, alleluia!

~BY THE WOOD OF THE CROSS, JOY CAME INTO THE
WHOLE WORLD.

Glory to the Father, and to the Son, and to the
    Holy Spirit:

~BY THE WOOD OF THE CROSS, JOY CAME INTO THE
WHOLE WORLD.

as it was in the beginning, is now, and will be
    forever. Amen.

ANTIPHON ~WE ADORE YOUR CROSS, O LORD,
AND WE PRAISE AND GLORIFY YOUR HOLY
RESURRECTION; BY THE WOOD OF THE CROSS, JOY
CAME INTO THE WHOLE WORLD.

LITANY
Lord Jesus, you died for our sins,
    and rose for our justification:

~Hear us, risen Lord.

Lord Jesus, you mastered death by your death,
   and brought life to those in the grave:
~Hear us, risen Lord.

Lord Jesus, you overcame death's sting
   and gave fresh life to a fallen world:
~Hear us, risen Lord.

Lord Jesus, you delivered our ancestors in the
   faith from the world of the dead:
~Hear us, risen Lord.

Lord Jesus, raise us from the tomb of our sins
   and offenses:
~Hear us, risen Lord.

Lord Jesus, give life to all those who fall asleep
   in you:
~Hear us, risen Lord.

(Offer spontaneous prayers of intercession.)

By the prayers of the great Mother of God,
   Mary most holy, and of all the saints in heaven:
~Hear us, risen Lord.

The Lord's Prayer

Closing Prayer
Abba, dear Father,
by our holy baptism
you buried us with Christ in death
and raised us to new life in the Spirit.

The Fifty Days of Easter **153**

Absolve us from all our sins,
give us again the joy of your help,
and sustain us with a spirit of fervor.
We ask this through the new Adam,
Jesus Christ, your Son,
whom you raised from the dead.
~AMEN.

Let us bless the Lord, alleluia, alleluia!
~THANKS BE TO GOD, ALLELUIA, ALLELUIA!

May the grace of our Lord Jesus Christ,
and the love of God,
and the communion of the Holy Spirit,
† be with us all, now and forever.
~AMEN.

For Use on the Tuesdays and Thursdays of Eastertide

Christ is risen from the tomb, alleluia, alleluia!
~FOR OUR SAKE HE HUNG ON THE CROSS, ALLELUIA,
ALLELUIA!

HYMN   EASTER TRIUMPH

At the Lamb's high feast we sing
praise to our victorious King.
He has washed us in the tide
flowing from his wounded side.
Praise the Lord whose love divine
gives his sacred blood for wine,

gives his body for the feast,
Christ the victim, Christ the priest.

Where the paschal blood is poured,
Death's dark angel sheathes his sword;
Israel's hosts triumphant go
through the wave that drowns the foe.
Christ the Lamb whose blood was shed,
paschal victim, paschal bread!
With sincerity and love
eat we manna from above.

Mighty victim from the sky,
powers of hell before you lie;
death is conquered in the fight,
you have brought us life and light.
Your victorious banners wave;
you have risen from the grave;
you have opened paradise,
and in you all saints shall rise.

Easter triumph, Easter joy,
this alone can sin destroy;
from the death of sin set free,
souls reborn, O Lord, we'll be.
Hymns of glory, songs of praise,
Father, unto you we raise;
and to you, our risen King,
with the Spirit, praise we sing.[69]

PSALM 118:1, 4–9,
13–17, 22–27　　　　　　**THE DAY OF DAYS**

ANTIPHON THIS DAY WAS MADE BY THE LORD;
LET US REJOICE AND BE GLAD, ALLELUIA!

Give thanks to the LORD who is good,
for God's love endures forever.
Let those who fear the LORD say:
"God's love endures forever."

~THIS DAY WAS MADE BY THE LORD;
LET US REJOICE AND BE GLAD, ALLELUIA!

I called to the LORD in my distress;
God answered and freed me.
The LORD is at my side; I do not fear.
What can mortals do against me?
The LORD is at my side as my helper;
I shall look down on my foes.

~THIS DAY WAS MADE BY THE LORD;
LET US REJOICE AND BE GLAD, ALLELUIA!

It is better to take refuge in the LORD
than to trust in mortals;
it is better to take refuge in the LORD
than to trust in rulers.

~THIS DAY WAS MADE BY THE LORD;
LET US REJOICE AND BE GLAD, ALLELUIA!

I was thrust down and falling,
but the LORD was my helper.
The LORD is my strength and my song;
and has been my savior.

156 The Fifty Days of Easter

There are shouts of joy and victory
in the tents of the just.

~THIS DAY WAS MADE BY THE LORD;
LET US REJOICE AND BE GLAD, ALLELUIA!

The LORD's right hand has triumphed;
God's right hand raised me.
The LORD's right hand has triumphed;
I shall not die, I shall live
and recount God's deeds.

~THIS DAY WAS MADE BY THE LORD;
LET US REJOICE AND BE GLAD, ALLELUIA!

The stone which the builders rejected
has become the cornerstone.
This is the work of the LORD,
a marvel in our eyes.

~THIS DAY WAS MADE BY THE LORD;
LET US REJOICE AND BE GLAD, ALLELUIA!

O LORD, grant us salvation;
O LORD, grant success.
We bless you from the house of the LORD;
the LORD God is our light.

~THIS DAY WAS MADE BY THE LORD;
LET US REJOICE AND BE GLAD, ALLELUIA!

Glory to the Father, and to the Son, and to the
  Holy Spirit:

~THIS DAY WAS MADE BY THE LORD;
LET US REJOICE AND BE GLAD, ALLELUIA!

as it was in the beginning, is now, and will be
   forever. Amen.

~THIS DAY WAS MADE BY THE LORD;
LET US REJOICE AND BE GLAD, ALLELUIA!

PSALM PRAYER
Let us pray *(pause for quiet prayer)*:

Abba, dear Father,
by the risen Christ whom we praise,
who slept that we might keep watch
and who died that we might live,
grant us the grace to reign with him
in the life that knows no end;
through the same Christ our Lord.
~AMEN.

READING   **NEW BIRTH**   **1 PETER 1:3–5**
Blessed be the God and Father of our Lord Jesus
Christ! By his great mercy he has given us a new
birth into a living hope through the resurrection
of Jesus Christ from the dead, and into an
inheritance that is imperishable, undefiled, and
unfading, kept in heaven for you, who are being
protected by the power of God through faith for a
salvation ready to be revealed in the last time.

(Pause for meditation.)

Thanks be to God who gives us the victory,
  alleluia!

~THROUGH OUR LORD JESUS CHRIST, ALLELUIA!

THE GREAT CANON OF ST. JOHN OF DAMASCUS

ANTIPHON CHRIST IS RISEN FROM THE DEAD,
CONQUERING DEATH BY DEATH,
AND GIVING LIFE TO THOSE IN THE GRAVE.

O Day of Resurrection!
Let us beam with festive joy!
Today indeed is the Lord's own Passover,
For from death to life, from earth to heaven,
Christ has led us
As we shout the victory hymn!

~CHRIST IS RISEN FROM THE DEAD,
CONQUERING DEATH BY DEATH,
AND GIVING LIFE TO THOSE IN THE GRAVE.

Let our hearts be spotless
As we gaze upon our dazzling Christ:
See his rising—a brilliant flash of light divine!
Let us listen,
clearly hear him greeting us,
As we shout the victory hymn!

~CHRIST IS RISEN FROM THE DEAD,
CONQUERING DEATH BY DEATH,
AND GIVING LIFE TO THOSE IN THE GRAVE.

Let all heaven burst with joy!
Let all earth resound with gladness!
Let all creation dance in celebration!
For Christ is risen:
Christ, our lasting joy!

~CHRIST IS RISEN FROM THE DEAD,
CONQUERING DEATH BY DEATH,
AND GIVING LIFE TO THOSE IN THE GRAVE.[70]

LITANY OF THE VICTORIOUS CROSS

Holy God, holy mighty One, holy immortal One,
~HAVE MERCY ON US.

We adore you, Lord Jesus Christ, as you ascend
your cross.
~MAY THIS CROSS DELIVER US FROM THE DESTROYING
ANGEL.

We adore your pierced and wounded body
hanging on the cross.
~MAY YOUR WOUNDS BE OUR HEALING.

We adore you dead and buried in the rock-hewn
tomb.
~MAY YOUR DEATH BE OUR LIFE.

We adore you as you descend among the dead
to deliver them.
~MAY WE NEVER HEAR THE DREAD SENTENCE OF
DOOM.

We adore you rising gloriously from the dead
and appearing to Mary Magdalene.
~FREE US FROM THE WEIGHT OF OUR SINS.

We adore you ascending to the right hand
of the Father.
~Raise us to eternal glory with all your saints.

We adore you coming to judge the living
and the dead.
~At your coming be not our Judge but our
Savior.

Holy God, holy mighty One, holy immortal One,
~Have mercy on us.[71]

THE LORD'S PRAYER

CLOSING PRAYER
Holy, mighty, and living God,
joy came into the world
when you lifted up your dear Son
from among the dead.
By the prayers of Mary his mother,
of the beloved disciple,
and of all the spice-bearing women,
raise us up with Jesus
and bring us to the happiness of everlasting life;
through the same Christ our Lord.
~Amen.[72]

Let us bless the Lord, alleluia, alleluia!
~Thanks be to God, alleluia, alleluia!

By the precious and life-giving cross,
may our risen Lord ✝ save and deliver us.
~Amen.

The *Via Lucis*

Just as we walk the way of the cross during Lent in order to meditate on the sufferings of Jesus, so we may walk the way of light *(Via Lucis)* during Eastertide in order to meditate on the glories of his resurrection. His dazzling appearances during the great fifty days reveal the awe, doubt, confusion, embarrassment, and conviction that dawned on the disciples, formed them, and prepared them for the coming of the Holy Spirit on the Day of Pentecost. These devotions might be extended over the seven weeks of Eastertide or used as a whole as in the case of the way of the cross.

We adore your cross, O Lord,
~AND WE PRAISE AND GLORIFY YOUR HOLY RESURRECTION, FOR BY THE WOOD OF THE CROSS, JOY CAME INTO THE WHOLE WORLD.

HYMN   **THE RISEN LORD**

A brightness glows o'er all the land
while joyful songs declare
that Jesus Christ confounded death
and freed us from despair.

The earth and sky, the Roman guards,
the tomb of solid stone,
could not but quake in helplessness
when Christ's true glory shone.

For thorns and wounds could never dim
the splendor of his might;
behold, he stands before us now
transfigured in our sight.

His followers were sorrowful,
confused, and filled with dread,
until they saw their risen Lord,
the firstborn of the dead.

We beg you now, O risen Lord,
direct your faithful friends,
defend us all from Satan's schemes,
receive us when life ends.[73]

1. Easter Morning

This day was made by the Lord, alleluia!
~WE REJOICE AND ARE GLAD, ALLELUIA.

READING   **EASTER MORNING**   **LUKE 24:1–11**

On the first day of the week, at early dawn, the
women who had followed Jesus from Galilee
came to the tomb, taking the spices that they had
prepared. They found the stone rolled away from
the tomb, but when they went in, they did not
find the body. While they were perplexed about
this, suddenly two men in dazzling clothes stood
beside them. The women were terrified and
bowed their faces to the ground, but the men said
to them, "Why do you look for the living among
the dead? He is not here, but has risen.
Remember how he told you, while he was still in
Galilee, that the Son of Man must be handed over
to sinners, and be crucified, and on the third day
rise again." Then they remembered his words,
and returning from the tomb, they told all this to

The Fifty Days of Easter **163**

the eleven and to all the rest. Now it was Mary Magdalene, Joanna, Mary the mother of James, and the other women with them who told this to the apostles. But these words seemed to them an idle tale, and they did not believe them.

(Pause for silent prayer.)

RESPONSE
Let all creation dance in celebration, alleluia!
~FOR CHRIST HAS RISEN, CHRIST OUR LASTING JOY, ALLELUIA!

PRAYER
Holy and wonderful God,
you so loved the world
that you sent your only Son
so that anyone who believes in him
may not perish but have eternal life.
As we remember all that was done for us,
the cross, the tomb, the resurrection
on the third day,
the ascension into heaven,
the enthronement at the right hand of the Father,
and the gift of the Holy Spirit,
may we offer fitting and grateful praise to you,
now and always and forever and ever.
~AMEN.

2. Easter Morning

This day was made by the Lord, alleluia!
~WE REJOICE AND ARE GLAD, ALLELUIA.

	THE FIRST DAY	
READING	**OF THE WEEK**	**JOHN 20:1–10**

Early on the first day of the week, while it was still dark, Mary Magdalene came to the tomb and saw that the stone had been removed from the tomb. So she ran and went to Simon Peter and the other disciple, the one whom Jesus loved, and said to them, "They have taken the Lord out of the tomb, and we do not know where they have laid him." Then Peter and the other disciple set out and went toward the tomb. The two were running together, but the other disciple outran Peter and reached the tomb first. He bent down to look in and saw the linen wrappings lying there, but he did not go in. Then Simon Peter came, following him, and went into the tomb. He saw the linen wrappings lying there, and the cloth that had been on Jesus' head, not lying with the linen wrappings but rolled up in a place by itself. Then the other disciple also went in, and he saw and believed; for as yet they did not understand the scripture, that he must rise from the dead. Then the disciples returned to their homes.

(Pause for silent prayer.)

The Lord's right hand has triumphed, alleluia!
~GOD'S RIGHT HAND HAS RAISED ME, ALLELUIA!

PRAYER
God of peace,
you brought our Lord Jesus back from the dead
to become the great Shepherd of the sheep
by the blood that sealed an eternal covenant.
Make us complete in everything good
so that we do his will, working among us
whatever is pleasing in his sight,
through Jesus Christ, to whom be the glory
forever and ever.
~AMEN.

3. Easter Afternoon

This day was made by the Lord, alleluia!
~WE REJOICE AND ARE GLAD, ALLELUIA.

READING   MARY MAGDALENE   JOHN 20:11–18
Mary stood weeping outside the tomb. As she
wept, she bent over to look into the tomb; and
she saw two angels in white, sitting where the
body of Jesus had been lying, one at the head and
the other at the feet. They said to her, "Woman
why are you weeping?" She said to them, "They
have taken away my Lord, and I do not know
where they have laid him." When she had said
this, she turned around and saw Jesus standing

there, but she did not know that it was Jesus.
Jesus said to her, "Woman, why are you weeping?
Whom are you looking for?" Supposing him to be
the gardener, she said to him, "Sir, if you have
carried him away, tell me where you have laid
him, and I will take him away." Jesus said to her,
"Mary!" She turned and said to him in Hebrew,
"Rabbouni!" (which means Teacher). Jesus said to
her, "Do not hold on to me, because I have not
yet ascended to the Father. But go to my brothers
and say to them, 'I am ascending to my Father
and your Father, to my God and your God.'"
Mary Magdalene went and announced to the disciples, "I have seen the Lord"; and she told them
that he had said these things to her.

(Pause for silent prayer.)

RESPONSE
The Lord is my strength and my song, alleluia!
~AND HAS BEEN MY SAVIOR, ALLELUIA!

PRAYER
Lord Jesus,
you rose from the dead
and testified to those who cherished you
that you were the life and light of the world.
May the witness and prayers of Mary Magdalene,
the apostle of the apostles,
fill our hearts with apostolic faith
to help and heal a sinful world.

We ask this through Christ our Lord.
~Amen.

4. Easter Evening
This day was made by the Lord, alleluia!
~We rejoice and are glad, alleluia.

The Emmaus Encounter

Reading   **Luke 24:13–27**

Now on that same day two of them were going to a village called Emmaus, about seven miles from Jerusalem, and talking with each other about all these things that had happened. While they were talking and discussing, Jesus himself came near and went with them, but their eyes were kept from recognizing him. And he said to them, "What are you discussing with each other while you walk along?" They stood still, looking sad. Then one of them, whose name was Cleopas, answered him, "Are you the only stranger in Jerusalem who does not know the things that have taken place there in these days?" He asked them, "What things?" They replied, "The things about Jesus of Nazareth, who was a prophet mighty in deed and word before God and all the people, and how our chief priests and leaders handed him over to be condemned to death and crucified him. But we had hoped that he was the one to redeem Israel. Yes, and besides all this, it is now the third day since these things took place. Moreover, some women of our group astounded us. They were at the tomb early this morning, and when they did not find his body there, they came back and told us that they had indeed seen a vision of angels who said that he was alive. Some of those who were with us went to the tomb and found it just as the women had said; but they did not see him." Then he said to them, "Oh, how foolish you are, and how slow of heart to believe all that the prophets have declared! Was it not necessary that the Messiah should suffer these things and then enter into his glory?" Then beginning with Moses and all the prophets, he interpreted to them the things about himself in all the scriptures.

(Pause for silent prayer.)

RESPONSE

The stone which the builders rejected, alleluia!
~HAS BECOME THE CORNERSTONE, ALLELUIA!

PRAYER

God of the prophets and seers of Israel,
you prepared a way for the coming of your Son
who was to suffer and to die for us
and so enter into his glory.
Help us to grasp the fuller meaning
of Moses and all the prophets of Israel
as they are revealed to us
in the newness of the paschal mystery
accomplished in our blessed Savior.

The Fifty Days of Easter **169**

We ask this in Jesus' name.
~AMEN.

5. Easter Evening

This day was made by the Lord, alleluia!
~WE REJOICE AND ARE GLAD, ALLELUIA.

THE EMMAUS

READING   **ENCOUNTER**   **LUKE 24:28–35**

As they came near the village to which they were
going, he walked ahead as if he were going on. But
they urged him strongly, saying, "Stay with us,
because it is almost evening and the day is now
nearly over." So he went in to stay with them. When
he was at the table with them, he took bread,
blessed and broke it, and gave it to them. Then
their eyes were opened, and they recognized him;
and he vanished from their sight. They said to each
other, "Were not our hearts burning within us
while he was talking to us on the road, while he was
opening the scriptures to us?" That same hour they
got up and returned to Jerusalem; and they found
the eleven and their companions gathered together.
They were saying, "The Lord has risen indeed, and
he has appeared to Simon!" Then they told what
had happened on the road, and how he had been
made known to them in the breaking of the bread.

(Pause for silent prayer.)

RESPONSE

Christ died for our sins and was buried, alleluia!

~AND WAS RAISED TO LIFE ON THE THIRD DAY,
ALLELUIA!

PRAYER

Father of our Lord Jesus Christ,
your risen Son revealed himself
to his chosen disciples
by interpreting the Scriptures for them
and in the breaking of the bread.
Reveal now to your Church at prayer
the Jesus of the Gospels and the Jesus of the
Eucharist
that our joy and understanding may be complete
in him who is Lord forever.

~AMEN.

6. Easter Evening

This day was made by the Lord, alleluia!

~WE REJOICE AND ARE GLAD, ALLELUIA.

| READING | RECEIVE THE HOLY SPIRIT | JOHN 20:19–25 |

When it was evening on that day, the first day of
the week, and the doors of the house where the
disciples had met were locked for fear of the Jews,
Jesus came and stood among them and said, "Peace
be with you." After he said this, he showed them
his hands and his side. Then the disciples rejoiced
when they saw the Lord. Jesus said to them again,

"Peace be with you. As the Father has sent me, so I send you." When he had said this, he breathed on them and said to them, "Receive the Holy Spirit. If you forgive the sins of any, they are forgiven them; if you retain the sins of any, they are retained."

But Thomas (who was called the Twin), one of the twelve, was not with them when Jesus came. So the other disciples told him, "We have seen the Lord." But he said to them, "Unless I see the mark of the nails in his hands, and put my finger in the mark of the nails and my hand in his side, I will not believe."

(Pause for silent prayer.)

RESPONSE

We adore your cross, O Lord, alleluia!
~AND WE PRAISE AND GLORIFY YOUR HOLY
    RESURRECTION, ALLELUIA!

PRAYER

God of peace and reconciliation,
the sight of Jesus' five precious wounds
filled the disciples with the joy of recognition
and prepared them for the gift of the Spirit.
Warm our cold hearts at the fire of your love
and fill us with the faith and joy
your dear Son won for us
by his suffering, death, and glorious resurrection.
We ask this through Christ our Lord.
~AMEN.

7. A Week Later

This day was made by the Lord, alleluia!

~We rejoice and are glad, alleluia.

Reading   My Lord and my God!   John 20:26–31

A week later his disciples were again in the house, and Thomas was with them. Although the doors were shut, Jesus came and stood among them and said, "Peace be with you." Then he said to Thomas, "Put your finger here and see my hands. Reach out your hand and put it in my side. Do not doubt but believe." Thomas answered him, "My Lord and my God!" Jesus said to him, "Have you believed because you have seen me? Blessed are those who have not seen and yet have come to believe."

Now Jesus did many other signs in the presence of his disciples, which are not written in this book. But these are written so that you may come to believe that Jesus is the Messiah, the Son of God, and that through believing you may have life in his name.

(Pause for silent prayer.)

Response

If we die with Christ, alleluia!

~We shall also live with Christ, alleluia!

Prayer

Loving Savior,
you brought peace to the fearful heart

of your doubting disciple Thomas.
May we put the finger of faith
in your glorious wounds
so that by coming to believe,
even though we have not seen and touched your
   risen flesh,
we may have life in your blessed name,
now and forever.
~Amen.

Hymn   **Hail the Day That Sees Him Rise**
Love's redeeming work is done;
Fought the fight, the battle won:
Lo, our Sun's eclipse is o'er!
Lo, he sets in blood no more.

Vain the stone, the watch, the seal,
Christ has burst the gates of hell;
Death in vain forbids his rise;
Christ has opened Paradise.

Lives again our glorious King;
Where, O death, is now thy sting?
Dying once, he all doth save;
Where thy victory, O grave?

Charles Wesley (1707–1788)

8. Easter Evening Again
This day was made by the Lord, alleluia!
~We rejoice and are glad, alleluia.

READING **TOUCH ME AND SEE** LUKE 24:36–43

While they were talking about this [the Emmaus encounter], Jesus himself stood among them and said to them, "Peace be with you." They were startled and terrified, and thought that they were seeing a ghost. He said to them, "Why are you frightened, and why do doubts arise in your hearts? Look at my hands and my feet; see that it is I myself. Touch me and see; for a ghost does not have flesh and bones as you see I have." And when he had said this, he showed them his hands and his feet. While in their joy they were disbelieving and still wondering, he said to them, "Have you anything here to eat?" They gave him a piece of broiled fish, and he took it and ate in their presence.

(Pause for silent prayer.)

RESPONSE
Christ was raised from the dead, alleluia!
~BY THE GLORY OF THE FATHER, ALLELUIA!

PRAYER
Risen Lord,
your life and death have passed
over into the sacraments of the church,
the life-giving memorials of your presence.
In the Blessed Eucharist may we touch by faith
your risen body and its glorious wounds,
O Savior of the world,

living and reigning with the Father and the Spirit, now and forever.
~AMEN.

9. Easter Evening

This day was made by the Lord, alleluia!
~WE REJOICE AND ARE GLAD, ALLELUIA.

READING **UNDERSTANDING THE SCRIPTURES** **LUKE 24:44–49**

Jesus said to them, "These are my words that I spoke to you while I was still with you—that everything written about me in the law of Moses, the prophets, and the psalms must be fulfilled." Then he opened their minds to understand the scriptures, and he said to them, "Thus it is written, that the Messiah is to suffer and to rise from the dead on the third day, and that repentance and forgiveness of sins is to be proclaimed in his name to all nations, beginning from Jerusalem. You are witnesses of these things. And see I am sending upon you what my Father promised; so stay here in the city until you have been clothed with power from on high.

(Pause for silent prayer.)

RESPONSE

God has given us new birth into a living hope, alleluia!

~THROUGH THE RESURRECTION OF CHRIST FROM
   THE DEAD, ALLELUIA!

PRAYER
Lord Jesus Christ,
you were fastened with nails to the wood of the
   cross
and raised on high for all to see.
As the sun grew dark and the earth quaked,
you surrendered your spirit to your Father,
descended among the dead,
broke open the gates of hell,
and freed those bound in darkness.
As angel choirs rejoiced,
you were raised to life again on the third day,
mastering death by your own death,
and canceling the power of sin.
By these mighty deeds on our behalf,
rescue us from our blindness and tepidity,
inspire us anew by your Holy Spirit,
and lead us into a life of prayer and service
worthy of your awesome sacrifice,
O Savior of the world,
living and reigning, now and forever.
~AMEN.

10. By the Sea of Tiberias
This day was made by the Lord, alleluia!
~WE REJOICE AND ARE GLAD, ALLELUIA.

Jesus showed himself again to the disciples by the Sea of Tiberias; and he showed himself in this way. Gathered there together were Simon Peter, Thomas called the Twin, Nathanael of Cana in Galilee, the sons of Zebedee, and two others of his disciples. Simon Peter said to them, "I am going fishing." They said to him, "We will go with you." They went out and got into the boat, but that night they caught nothing.

Just after daybreak, Jesus stood on the beach; but the disciples did not know that it was Jesus. Jesus said to them, "Children, you have no fish, have you?" They answered him, "No." He said to them, "Cast the net to the right side of the boat, and you will find some." So they cast it, and now they were not able to haul it in because there were so many fish. That disciple whom Jesus loved said to Peter, "It is the Lord." When Simon Peter heard that it was the Lord, he put on some clothes, for he was naked, and jumped into the sea. But the other disciples came in the boat, dragging the net full of fish, for they were not far from the land, only about a hundred yards off.

(Pause for silent prayer.)

RESPONSE

God raised Christ from the dead, alleluia!

~AND SET HIM FREE FROM THE PAINS OF DEATH, ALLELUIA!

PRAYER

Lord of glory,
you gathered your friends at the Lake of Galilee
and had them witness your risen life.
May we eat and drink with you
and become living witnesses
to the reign of God in our lives.
You live and reign, now and forever.
~AMEN.

11. Bread and Fish

This day was made by the Lord, alleluia!
~WE REJOICE AND ARE GLAD, ALLELUIA.

READING   **AT THE SEA OF TIBERIAS, CONTINUED**   JOHN 21:9–14

When they had gone ashore, they saw a charcoal fire there, with fish on it, and bread. Jesus said to them, "Bring some of the fish that you have just caught." So Simon Peter went aboard and hauled the net ashore, full of large fish, a hundred fifty-three of them; and though there were so many, the net was not torn. Jesus said to them, "Come and have breakfast." Now none of the disciples dared to ask him, "Who are you?" because they knew it was the Lord. Jesus came and took the bread and gave it to them, and did the same with the fish. This was now the third time that Jesus appeared to the disciples after he was raised from the dead.

(Pause for silent prayer.)

RESPONSE

Thanks be to God who gives us the victory,
alleluia!

~THROUGH OUR LORD JESUS CHRIST, ALLELUIA!

PRAYER

Christ Jesus,
host of the Galilean breakfast,
have us recognize you each Lord's Day
as we share in the breaking of the bread
and the pouring of the wine
in the eucharistic banquet
of your precious Body and Blood,
the indelible signs of love made visible.
Blessed be Jesus in the sacrament of the altar!
~AMEN.

12. Simon Peter

This day was made by the Lord, alleluia!
~WE REJOICE AND ARE GLAD, ALLELUIA.

READING **AT THE SEA OF TIBERIAS, CONTINUED** **JOHN 21:15–19**

When they had finished breakfast, Jesus said to
Simon Peter, "Simon son of John, do you love me
more than these?" He said to him, "Yes, Lord; you
know that I love you." Jesus said to him, "Feed my
lambs." A second time he said to him, "Simon son
of John, do you love me?" He said to him, "Yes,

Lord; you know that I love you." Jesus said to him, "Tend my sheep." He said to him the third time, "Simon son of John, do you love me?" Peter felt hurt because he said to him the third time, "Do you love me?" And he said to him, "Lord, you know everything; you know that I love you." Jesus said to him "Feed my sheep. Very truly, I tell you, when you were younger, you used to fasten your own belt and go wherever you wished. But when you grow old, you will stretch out your hands, and someone else will fasten a belt around you and take you where you do not wish to go." (He said this to indicate the kind of death by which he would glorify God.) After this he said to him, "Follow me."

(Pause for silent prayer.)

RESPONSE
The Lord is risen indeed, alleluia!
~AND HAS APPEARED TO SIMON PETER, ALLELUIA!

PRAYER
Most High God,
vacillating and impetuous Simon
learned to repent of his betrayal,
shed tears of remorse,
and become your loving disciple again.
By his example and prayers,
turn our hard hearts to you
and teach us to love and cherish
the lambs and sheep of your flock.

We ask this through Christ, the good Shepherd.
~AMEN.

13. Galilee Again

This day was made by the Lord, alleluia!
~WE REJOICE AND ARE GLAD, ALLELUIA.

READING | THE GREAT COMMISSION | MATTHEW 28:16–20

Now the eleven disciples went to Galilee, to the mountain to which Jesus had directed them. When they saw him, they worshiped him; but some doubted. And Jesus came and said to them, "All authority in heaven and on earth has been given to me. Go therefore and make disciples of all nations, baptizing them in the name of the Father and of the Son and of the Holy Spirit, and teaching them to obey everything that I have commanded you. And remember, I am with you always, to the end of the age."

(Pause for silent prayer.)

RESPONSE

God goes up with shouts of joy, alleluia!
~THE LORD GOES UP WITH TRUMPET BLAST, ALLELUIA!

PRAYER

God our Savior,
you heard your Son when he cried out
in pain and humiliation on the cross
and raised him up out of the sleep of death.

By the power of his resurrection and ascension,
uphold your people, shield us from our enemies,
and bring us home in safety at the last.
We ask this through the same Christ our Lord.
~AMEN.

14. The Final Day on Earth

This day was made by the Lord, alleluia!
~WE REJOICE AND ARE GLAD, ALLELUIA.

READING   **THE ASCENSION**   **LUKE 24:50–53**

Jesus led them out as far as Bethany, and, lifting
up his hands, he blessed them. While he was
blessing them, he withdrew from them and was
carried up into heaven. And they worshiped him,
and returned to Jerusalem with great joy; and
they were continually in the temple blessing God.

(Pause for silent prayer.)

RESPONSE

You will be my witnesses in Jerusalem, alleluia!
~AND TO THE ENDS OF THE EARTH, ALLELUIA!

PRAYER

God of fire and light,
on the first Pentecost you formed the hearts
of those who believed in you
by the indwelling of the Holy Spirit:
Under the inspiration of that same Spirit,
give us a taste for what is right and true

and a continuing sense of his joy-bringing
presence and power.
We ask this through Christ our Lord.
~AMEN.

May the grace of our Lord Jesus Christ,
and the love of God, and the communion of the
    Holy Spirit,
† be with us all, now and forever.
~AMEN.

A Novena for Pentecost

*Eastertide concludes with Pentecost Sunday,
the fiftieth day, and commemorates the first out-
pouring of the Holy Spirit (Acts 2:1–4), the
Church's foundation, and the beginning of its
mission to all nations and all peoples. The mystery of Pentecost exhorts us to prayer and commitment to mission and enlightens popular piety,
which is a "continued sign of the presence of the
Holy Spirit in the Church."* [74]

*The original nine days of prayer—from which
all novenas derive—are those between the Feast
of Ascension Thursday and Pentecost Sunday
when Mary, the apostles, and Jesus' brothers
continued together in prayer in the upper room
until they were "clothed with power from on high"
(Acts 1:14; Luke 24:49). We rejoice in the coming
of the Spirit of truth and consolation, and we pray
for an increase of the holy gifts with which the
Spirit endows the Church. We pray too for the
reform and renewal of the Church, its institutions,*

and its attitudes. We also ask for the seven gifts of the Holy Spirit and for personal renewal and refreshment. The seven gifts of the Holy Spirit traditionally recognized as such by the Church are these: wisdom, understanding, counsel, fortitude, knowledge, piety, and fear of the Lord (see Isaiah 11:1–3).

Come, Holy Spirit, fill the hearts of your faithful,
~AND KINDLE IN THEM THE FIRE OF YOUR LOVE.

HYMN TO THE HOLY SPIRIT

O Holy Spirit, by whose breath
life rises vibrant out of death:
come to create, renew, inspire;
come, kindle in our hearts your fire.

You are the seeker's sure resource,
of burning love the living source,
protector in the midst of strife,
the giver and the Lord of life.

In you God's energy is shown,
to us your varied gifts made known.
Teach us to speak, teach us to hear;
yours is the tongue and yours the ear.

Flood our dull senses with your light;
in mutual love our hearts unite.
Your power the whole creation fills;
confirm our weak, uncertain wills.

From inner strife grant us release;
turn nations to the ways of peace;

to fuller life your people bring
that as one body we may sing:

Praise to the Father, Christ his Word,
and to the Spirit, God the Lord;
to them all honor, glory be
both now and in eternity.
Amen.[75]

PSALM 33:12–15, 18–22   GOD'S LOVE IS UPON US

ANTIPHON   THE LORD'S SPIRIT FILLS THE ENTIRE WORLD
AND HOLDS EVERYTHING IN IT TOGETHER.

They are happy, whose God is the LORD,
the people who are chosen as his own.
From the heavens the LORD looks forth
and sees all the peoples of the earth.

~THE LORD'S SPIRIT FILLS THE ENTIRE WORLD
AND HOLDS EVERYTHING IN IT TOGETHER.

From the heavenly dwelling God gazes
on all the dwellers on the earth;
God who shapes the hearts of them all
and considers all their deeds.

~THE LORD'S SPIRIT FILLS THE ENTIRE WORLD
AND HOLDS EVERYTHING IN IT TOGETHER.

The LORD looks on those who fear him,
on those who hope in his love,
to rescue their souls from death,
to keep them alive in famine.

~THE LORD'S SPIRIT FILLS THE ENTIRE WORLD
AND HOLDS EVERYTHING IN IT TOGETHER.

Our soul is waiting for the LORD.
He is our help and our shield.
Our heart finds joy in him.
We trust in his holy name.

~THE LORD'S SPIRIT FILLS THE ENTIRE WORLD
AND HOLDS EVERYTHING IN IT TOGETHER.

May your love be upon us, O LORD,
as we place all our hope in you.

~THE LORD'S SPIRIT FILLS THE ENTIRE WORLD
AND HOLDS EVERYTHING IN IT TOGETHER.

PSALM PRAYER

Let us pray *(pause for quiet prayer)*:

Heavenly King, Consoler, Spirit of truth,
present in all places, filling all things,
treasury of blessings and giver of life:
Come and dwell in us,
cleanse us from every stain of sin
and save our souls,
O gracious Lord.

~AMEN.

READING   GOD'S CHILDREN   ROMANS 8:14–17[76]

Those who are led by God's Spirit are God's children. For the Spirit that God has given you does
not make you slaves and cause you to be afraid;
instead, the Spirit makes you God's children, and

by the Spirit's power we cry out to God, "Father!
my Father!" God's Spirit joins himself to our spirits to declare that we are God's children. Since we
are his children, we will possess the blessings he
keeps for his people, and we will also possess with
Christ what God has kept for him; for if we share
Christ's suffering, we will also share his glory.

SILENCE

RESPONSE
Be filled with the Spirit, alleluia!
~SING HYMNS AND PSALMS IN YOUR HEARTS, ALLELUIA!

THE GOLDEN SEQUENCE
Holy Spirit, font of light,
focus of God's glory bright,
shed on us a shining ray.

Father of the fatherless,
giver of gifts limitless,
come and touch our hearts today.

Source of strength and sure relief,
comforter in time of grief,
enter in and be our guest.

On our journey grant us aid,
freshening breeze and cooling shade,
in our labor inward rest.

Enter each aspiring heart,
occupy its inmost part,
with your dazzling purity.

All that gives to us our worth,
all that benefits the earth,
you bring to maturity.

With your soft refreshing rains,
break our drought, remove our stains;
bind up all our injuries.

Shake with rushing wind our will;
melt with fire our icy chill;
bring to light our perjuries.

As your promise we believe
make us ready to receive
gifts from your unbounded store.

Grant enabling energy,
courage in adversity,
joys that last forevermore.
Amen.[77]

LITANY OF THE HOLY SPIRIT

Lord and life-giving Spirit, in the beginning you
    brooded over the primeval waters.

~COME, FILL OUR HEARTS.

You led your people out of slavery and into the
    freedom of the children of God.

~COME, FILL OUR HEARTS.

You overshadowed Mary of Nazareth and made her
    the Mother of God.

~COME, FILL OUR HEARTS.

You anointed Jesus as Messiah when he was
   baptized by John in the Jordan.
~COME, FILL OUR HEARTS.

You raised Jesus out of death and proclaimed him
   Son of God in all his power.
~COME, FILL OUR HEARTS.

You appeared in tongues of flame on Pentecost
   and endowed your Church
   with charismatic gifts.
~COME, FILL OUR HEARTS.

You send us out to testify to the Good News
   of Jesus Christ.
~COME, FILL OUR HEARTS.

(Pause for special intentions.)

THE LORD'S PRAYER

CLOSING PRAYER
Come, Holy Spirit, come!
Come as holy fire and burn in us,
come as holy wind and cleanse us,
come as holy light and lead us,
come as holy truth and teach us,
come as holy forgiveness and free us,
come as holy love and enfold us,
come as holy power and enable us,
come as holy life and dwell in us,
convict us, convert us, consecrate us,
until we are wholly yours for your using,

through Jesus Christ our Lord.
~AMEN.[78]

May the grace of our Lord Jesus Christ
and the love of God
and the communion of the Holy Spirit
✝ be with us all, now and forever.
~AMEN.

Post-Pentecostal Solemnities

Thanks to the growth of popular piety in the late Middle Ages and in modern times, three eminent forms of devotion entered the Liturgy to become the solemnities of the Holy Trinity, Corpus Christi, and the Sacred Heart of Jesus. As well as on the feasts themselves, these devotions may be used at any time of the year as personal piety suggests.

A Devotion in Honor of the Holy Trinity

A Trinitarian orientation is an essential element in popular piety. . . . All pious exercises in honor of the Blessed Virgin Mary and of the Angels and Saints have the Father as their final end, from whom all things come and to whom all things return; the incarnate, dead, and resurrected Son is the only mediator (1 Timothy 2:5) apart from whom access to the Father is impossible (John 14:6); the Holy Spirit is the only source of grace and sanctification.[79]

Devotion to the Trinity grew out of private devotion based on the many Trinitarian formulas in the liturgy—the lesser Doxology ("Glory to the

193

*Father and to the Son and to the Holy Spirit . . .")
and the greater Doxology ("Glory to God in the
highest . . .")—and spread through the Latin West
during and after the ninth century. After the celebration proliferated for several centuries, Pope
John XXII extended the feast of the Blessed
Trinity to the whole Latin Church in 1334. It is celebrated on the first Sunday after Pentecost.*

In the name of the Father, † and of the Son,
and of the Holy Spirit.
~AMEN.

HYMN TO THE HOLY TRINITY

Eternal Trinity of love,
in peace and majesty you reign;
all things come forth from you alone;
to you they must return.

Creation lives and breathes in you,
sustained by your almighty will;
grant us to know you, God of truth,
in whom the questing mind is stilled.

Our Father, in the name of Christ,
unceasingly the Spirit send;
be with us everlasting God:
fulfil your purpose to the end.

We praise you, Godhead, One in Three,
immortal Trinity of light,
unchanging through eternal days
you live unmoved, serene in might.[80]

ANTIPHON GOD REIGNS IN BEAUTY, ALLELUIA!

The LORD is king, with majesty enrobed;
the LORD is robed with might,
and girded round with power.

The world you made firm, not to be moved;
your throne has stood firm from of old.
From all eternity, O Lord, you are.

The waters have lifted up, O LORD,
the waters have lifted up their voice,
the waters have lifted up their thunder.

Greater than the roar of mighty waters,
more glorious than the surgings of the sea,
the LORD is glorious on high.

Truly your decrees are to be trusted.
Holiness is fitting to your house,
O LORD, until the end of time.

ANTIPHON GOD REIGNS IN BEAUTY, ALLELUIA!

PSALM PRAYER
Let us pray *(pause for quiet prayer):*

Blessed and immortal Trinity,
mighty Father, only begotten Son, and Holy Spirit,
you are our first beginning and last end.
We praise, adore, and magnify you
and implore you to conduct us into endless bliss

with all the host of angels and the legion of saints
who worship you, now and forever.

~Amen.

READING   **THE DIVINE TRINITY**   **TITUS 3:4–7**[81]

When the kindness and love of God our Savior
was revealed, he saved us. It was not because of
any good deeds that we ourselves had done, but
because of his own mercy that he saved us,
through the Holy Spirit, who gives us new birth
and new life by washing us. God poured out the
Holy Spirit abundantly on us through Jesus
Christ our Savior, so that by his grace we might
be put right with God and come into possession
of the eternal life we hope for.

SILENCE

RESPONSE

Holy is God, holy and strong, holy and living
    forever:

~NOW AND ALWAYS AND FOREVER AND EVER. AMEN.

The Song of the Church (Te Deum)[82]

A. We praise you, O God,
we acclaim you as Lord;
all creation worships you,
the Father everlasting.

To you all angels, all the powers of heaven,
the cherubim and seraphim, sing in endless praise:

Holy, holy, holy Lord, God of power and might,
heaven and earth are full of your glory.

The glorious company of apostles praise you.
The noble fellowship of prophets praise you.
The white-robed army of martyrs praise you.

Throughout the world the holy Church
    acclaims you:
    Father, of majesty unbounded,
    your true and only Son, worthy of all praise,
    and the Holy Spirit, advocate and guide.

B. You, Christ, are the king of glory,
the eternal Son of the Father.
When you took our flesh to set us free
you humbly chose the Virgin's womb.

You overcame the sting of death
and opened the kingdom of heaven to all believers.
You are seated at God's right hand in glory.
We believe that you will come to be our judge.

Come then, Lord, and help your people,
bought with the price of your own blood,
and bring us with your saints
to glory everlasting.

C. Save your people, Lord, and bless your
    inheritance.
~GOVERN AND UPHOLD THEM NOW AND ALWAYS.

Day by day we bless you.
~WE PRAISE YOUR NAME FOR EVER.

Keep us today, Lord, from all sin.
~HAVE MERCY ON US, LORD, HAVE MERCY.

Lord, show us your love and mercy.
~FOR WE HAVE PUT OUR TRUST IN YOU.

In you, Lord, is our hope.
~LET US NEVER BE PUT TO SHAME.

LITANY OF THE HOLY TRINITY

Abba, merciful and compassionate Father:
~HAVE MERCY ON US.

Abba, Lord of the angelic messengers
   and of all the unearthly powers:
~HAVE MERCY ON US.

Abba, who redeemed the work of your hands
   by your only Son:
~HAVE MERCY ON US.

Lord Jesus, image of the invisible God
   and firstborn of all creation:
~HAVE MERCY ON US.

Lord Jesus, light of the angels
   and Savior of the human race:
~HAVE MERCY ON US.

Lord Jesus, the firstborn from the dead
   and head of your body, the Church:
~HAVE MERCY ON US.

Holy Spirit, advocate and guide of the faithful:
~HAVE MERCY ON US.

Holy Spirit, comforter and consoler of those
who mourn:
~HAVE MERCY ON US.

Holy Spirit, giver of life and teacher of truth:
~HAVE MERCY ON US.

(Pause for special intentions.)

THE LORD'S PRAYER

CLOSING PRAYER[83]
God, we praise you:
Father all-powerful, Christ Lord and Savior,
Spirit of love.
You reveal yourself in the depths of our being,
drawing us to share in your life and your love.
One God, three Persons,
be near to the people formed in your image,
close to the world your love brings to life.
We ask this, Father, Son, and Holy Spirit,
One God, true and living, forever and ever.
~AMEN.

May the grace of our Lord Jesus Christ
and the love of God
and the communion of the Holy Spirit
† be with us all.
~AMEN.

A Devotion to the Blessed Sacrament for Corpus Christi

Every Thursday of Holy Week, the Church celebrates the fact that, before his betrayal and death, Jesus washed the feet of his disciples and left us the supreme gift of the Eucharist during the Last Supper. It brings to completion the Jewish Passover meal and all the sacrifices of the old law of Moses. Thanks to Blessed Juliana of Mount Cornillon (1192–1258) and Blessed Eva of Liege (d. ca. 1265), a solemn Feast of the Blessed Sacrament was introduced into the city of Liege in 1264 and extended to the whole Latin Church by Pope Urban IV in 1264 in a text created by St. Thomas Aquinas, O.P. This solemnity is observed on the Thursday or Sunday following the feast of the Holy Trinity.

The renewed liturgy of the twentieth century has reconnected a more generous Liturgy of the Word to the Eucharistic sacrifice proper. It has also restored more frequent Holy Communion and communion in the form of both bread and wine for all.

Since very early on, churches reserved the Sacrament of the Altar for the sick and the dying (Viaticum), who are communicated from it in their homes, hospitals, and nursing homes. The reserved Sacrament is a sign of Christ's abiding presence with his people and has become a focal point for both private worship (visits to the Blessed Sacrament) and for public forms of meditation and veneration (Eucharistic processions, Benediction, Forty Hours, Holy Hours).

In the name of the Father, † and of the Son,
   and of the Holy Spirit.
~AMEN.

I am the living bread that came down from
heaven.
~IF YOU EAT THIS BREAD YOU WILL LIVE FOREVER.

Those who eat my flesh and drink my blood
~LIVE IN ME AND I IN THEM.

For my flesh is real food;
~MY BLOOD IS REAL DRINK.

A EUCHARISTIC HYMN

Jesus, Lord of glory, clothed in heaven's light,
here I bow before you, hidden from my sight.
King to whom my body, mind, and heart belong,
mind and heart here falter, Love so deep, so strong.

Here distrust, my spirit, eye and tongue and hand,
trust faith's ear and listen, hear and understand.
Hear the voice of Wisdom, speaking now to you;
when God's Word has spoken, what can be
more true?

Once you hid your glory, Jesus crucified;
now you hide your body, Jesus glorified.
When you come in judgment, plain for all to see,
God and man in splendor; Lord, remember me.

Once you showed to Thomas wounded hands
and side;
here I kneel adoring, faith alone my guide.
Help me grow in faith, Lord, grow in hope
and love,
living by your Spirit, gift of God above.

Here I see your dying, Jesus, victim-priest;
here I know your rising, host and guest and feast.
Let me taste your goodness, manna from the skies;
feed me, heal me, save me, food of Paradise.

Heart of Jesus, broken, pierced and opened wide,
wash me in the water flowing from your side.
Jesus' blood, so precious that one drop could free
all the world from evil, come and ransom me.

How I long to see you, Jesus, face to face,
how my heart is thirsting, living spring of grace.
Show me soon your glory, be my great reward,
be my joy forever, Jesus, gracious Lord.
Amen.[84]

PSALM 23   **SHEPHERD, HOST, AND FOOD**
ANTIPHON YOU HAVE PREPARED A BANQUET FOR ME.

LORD, you are my shepherd;
there is nothing I shall want.
Fresh and green are the pastures
where you give me repose.
Near restful waters you lead me,
to revive my drooping spirit.

You guide me along the right path;
you are true to your name.
If I should walk in the valley of darkness
no evil would I fear.
You are there with your crook and your staff;
with these you give me comfort.

You have prepared a banquet for me
in the sight of my foes.
My head you have anointed with oil;
my cup is overflowing.

Surely goodness and kindness shall follow me
all the days of my life.
In the LORD's own house shall I dwell
for ever and ever.

ANTIPHON YOU HAVE PREPARED A BANQUET FOR ME.

PSALM PRAYER
Let us pray *(pause for quiet prayer):*

Lord Jesus Christ,
shepherd of your Church,
you give us new birth in the waters of baptism,
anoint us with saving oil,
and call us to salvation at your holy table.
Dispel the terrors of death
and the darkness of error.
Lead your people along safe paths
that they may rest securely in you
and dwell forever in your Father's house,
where you live and reign forever and ever.
~AMEN.

READING **GOD'S NEW COVENANT** **1 CORINTHIANS 11:23–25**
I received from the Lord what I also handed on to
you, that the Lord Jesus on the night when he was
betrayed took a loaf of bread, and when he had

given thanks, he broke it and said, "This is my body that is for you. Do this in remembrance of me." In the same way he took the cup also, after supper, saying, "This cup is the new covenant in my blood. Do this, as often as you drink it, in remembrance of me."

SILENCE

RESPONSE

As often as you eat this bread and drink the cup,
~YOU PROCLAIM THE LORD'S DEATH UNTIL HE COMES.

CANTICLE OF THE VIRGIN MARY   **LUKE 1:46–55**

ANTIPHON HOW SACRED IS THE FEAST IN WHICH CHRIST IS OUR FOOD, THE MEMORIAL OF HIS PASSION IS CELEBRATED ANEW, OUR HEARTS ARE FILLED WITH GRACE, AND WE ARE GIVEN A PLEDGE OF THE GLORY WHICH IS TO COME, ALLELUIA!

My soul † proclaims the greatness of the Lord,
my spirit rejoices in God my Savior,
for you, Lord, have looked with favor
on your lowly servant.

From this day all generations will call me blessed:
 you, the Almighty, have done great things
   for me
 and holy is your name.
 You have mercy on those who fear you,
 from generation to generation.

You have shown strength with your arm
and scattered the proud in their conceit,
casting down the mighty from their thrones
and lifting up the lowly.
You have filled the hungry with good things
and sent the rich away empty.

You have come to the aid of your servant Israel,
to remember the promise of mercy,
the promise made to our forebears,
to Abraham and his children forever.

Glory to the Father, and to the Son,
and to the Holy Spirit:
as it was in the beginning, is now,
and will be forever. Amen.

ANTIPHON HOW SACRED IS THE FEAST IN WHICH
CHRIST IS OUR FOOD, THE MEMORIAL OF HIS PASSION
IS CELEBRATED ANEW, OUR HEARTS ARE FILLED WITH
GRACE, AND WE ARE GIVEN A PLEDGE OF THE GLORY
WHICH IS TO COME, ALLELUIA!

LITANY OF THE BLESSED SACRAMENT
(SEE PAGES 219–220)

OR THIS PRAYER:
Be present, be present, O Jesus,
great and good high priest:
Be present to us as you were
to your disciples at the Last Supper

and as you were made known
in the opening of the Scriptures
and in the breaking of bread
at Emmaus on Easter evening;
for yours is the power and the glory,
now and forever.
~AMEN.[85]

Those who come to me will never be hungry,
~THOSE WHO BELIEVE IN ME WILL NEVER BE THIRSTY.

May the Heart of Jesus
in the most Blessed Sacrament
be praised, adored, and loved
with grateful affection,
at every moment,
in all the tabernacles of the world,
even unto the end of time.
~AMEN.

A Devotion to the
Sacred Heart of Jesus

Many medieval saints and mystics were devoted to
the five wounds of Jesus and especially to the wound
in his side that was pierced by a soldier's lance and
poured forth blood and water (see John 19:34).
Blessed Julian of Norwich (c. 1342–1423) saw this
fifth wound in her famous *Showings*:

> *Very merrily and gladly our Lord looked into his*
> *side, and he gazed and said this: My child, if you*
> *cannot look on my divinity, see here how I suffered*

my side to be opened and my heart to be split in two and to send out blood and water, all that was in it; and this is a delight to me, and I wish it to be so for you.[86]

In the seventeenth century a group of three French saints fixed on the Sacred Heart of Jesus as the chief sign of God's love for us. They were Margaret Mary Alacoque (1647–1690), John Eudes (1601–1680), and Claude de la Colombiere, S.J. (1641–1682). Thanks to their vision and efforts, devotion to the Sacred Heart in the form of the Nine Fridays, the Holy Hour, and a new feast in honor of the Sacred Heart gradually spread throughout the Latin Church. This form of devotion was first officially recognized by Pope Clement XIII in 1765 and became a central form of piety in the nineteenth and twentieth centuries. In the United States the solemnity of the Sacred Heart is celebrated on the Friday following the second Sunday after Pentecost.

In the name of the Father, † and of the Son, and of the Holy Spirit.

~AMEN.

HYMN   THE GOD OF LOVE

The love of God is shown to all
in Christ our Savior's wounded heart;
he asks us now to share his cross
and in his passion take our part.

We are the Father's gift to Christ
who loved his own until the end;
his burden light we bear with joy,
and gladly to his yoke we bend.

Where love and loving-kindness are,
the God of love will always be;
with cords of love he binds us fast,
yet leaves the willing captive free.

Praise Father, Son, and Spirit blest,
Eternal Trinity sublime,
who make their home in humble hearts,
indwelling to the end of time.[87]

Psalm 36:5–11   God's Goodness

Antiphon O Lord, how precious is your love!

Your love, Lord, reaches to heaven,
your truth to the skies.
Your justice is like God's mountain,
your judgments like the deep.

To mortals and beasts you give protection.
O Lord, how precious is your love.
My God, the children of the earth
find refuge in the shadow of your wings.

They feast on the riches of your house;
they drink from the stream of your delight.
In you is the source of life,
and in your light we see light.

Keep on loving those who know you,
doing justice for upright hearts.
Let the foot of the proud not crush me
nor the hand of the wicked cast me out.

Antiphon O Lord, how precious is your love!

Psalm Prayer

Let us pray *(pause for quiet prayer)*:

Sacred Heart of Jesus,
how precious is your love for us.
Keep on loving those who know you,
and hide us in the shadow of your cross
as we seek your mercy and your help
in time of need.
You live and reign, now and forever.
~Amen.

Reading **The Gospel in Brief** **John 3:16, 35-36**

God so loved the world that he gave his only Son,
so that everyone who believes in him may not
perish but may have eternal life. The Father loves
the Son and has placed all things in his hand.
Whoever believes in the Son has eternal life; whoever disobeys the Son will not see life, but must
endure God's wrath.

Silence

Response

Take my yoke upon you and learn from me,
~For I am meek and humble of heart.

Canticle of St. Peter the Apostle **1 Peter 2:21-24**

Antiphon My yoke is easy, and my burden is light.

Christ suffered for us,
leaving us an example,
so that we should follow in his steps.

"He committed no sin,
and no deceit was found in his mouth."

When he was abused,
he did not return abuse;
when he suffered,
he did not threaten;
but he entrusted himself
to the One who judges justly.

He himself bore our sins
in his body on the cross,
so that, free from sins,
we might live for righteousness;
by his wounds
we have been healed.

ANTIPHON ~MY YOKE IS EASY, AND MY BURDEN
IS LIGHT.

LITANY OF THE SACRED HEART OF JESUS
(SEE PAGES 214–216)

OR THIS PRAYER
Jesus, Savior of the world,
in your Holy Gospel you tell us:
"Ask, and it will be given you; search, and you
will find;

knock, and the door will be opened for you"
(Matthew 7:7).
Moved by your divine promises,
I address you as my Savior,
whose heart is an inexhaustible source of grace.
Where else should I turn except to your infinite
mercy?
Where else should I knock except at the door
through which we go to God?
Sacred Heart of Jesus,
I put my whole trust in you,
the Lover of the human race,
the Consoler of the afflicted,
the Strength of those overwhelmed by their trials,
the Light of those who walk in darkness
or in the shadow of death.
You live and reign, now and forever.
~Amen.

May the Heart of Jesus
in the most Blessed Sacrament
be praised, adored, and loved
with grateful affection,
at every moment,
in all the tabernacles of the world,
even unto the end of time.
~Amen.

Litanies and Insistent Prayer

A litany is an ancient form of repetitive, insistent prayer originally designed for the Eucharistic Liturgy and the Daily Office and for certain liturgical processions (e.g., the Litany of the Saints). It was led by a deacon who formulated the petitions, and the congregation answered with a simple response: *"Kyrie, eleison"* ("Lord, have mercy") or "Lord, hear our prayer." The Second Vatican Council revived the use of litanies in the Eucharist and in daily Morning and Evening Prayer, and many Anglican and Protestant churches have followed suit. A litany helps us to pray earnestly and urgently for the Church and the world as a liturgical expression of Jesus' words: "Ask, and you will receive; seek, and you will find; knock, and the door will be opened to you" (Matthew 7:7 TEV).

In popular devotions the litany takes on new life as a beautiful and powerful form of intercessory prayer. Such litanies are forceful reminders of the central mysteries of the faith. In brief phrases from the Bible, the Liturgy, and Christian poetry, they bring to mind before God motives for faith, trust, devotion, love, and adoration as we ask for mercy and assistance. Good examples of such litanies are those of the Sacred Heart of Jesus, the Precious Blood of Jesus, the Blessed

Sacrament of the Altar, and the Blessed Virgin Mary. These litanies immerse us in the wonderful attributes of Jesus and Mary while we pray for some special intention. For example, when we offer one of the litanies of the Blessed Virgin, we recall her glorious role in our salvation while asking for her all-powerful intercession.

In addition to their use for intercession, litanies may be used as a form of mantra, a short phrase that helps focus prayer. Their beautiful and well-worn phrases become a kind of holy singsong to lull our wandering imagination and help us concentrate on God alone. In this sense they resemble the Rosary and the Jesus Prayer. Their holy monotony is their special attraction because they lead us beyond mere words to the very person of God who is ineffable, that is, radically incapable of being confined to human words. A triduum or novena often uses a litany as its form of intercession over three or nine days.

Litany of the Sacred Heart of Jesus

Lord, have mercy.	~LORD, HAVE MERCY.
Christ, have mercy.	~CHRIST, HAVE MERCY.
Lord, have mercy.	~LORD, HAVE MERCY.

God our Father in heaven,	~HAVE MERCY ON US.
God the Son, Redeemer of the world,	~HAVE MERCY ON US.
God the Holy Spirit,	~HAVE MERCY ON US.
Holy Trinity, one God,	~HAVE MERCY ON US.

Heart of Jesus, Son of the eternal Father,	~HAVE MERCY ON US.
Heart of Jesus, formed by the Holy Spirit in the womb of the Virgin Mother,	~HAVE MERCY ON US.
Heart of Jesus, one with the eternal Word,	~HAVE MERCY ON US.

Heart of Jesus, infinite in majesty, ~HAVE MERCY ON US.

Heart of Jesus, holy temple of God ~HAVE MERCY ON US.

Heart of Jesus, tabernacle of
the Most High, ~HAVE MERCY ON US.

Heart of Jesus, house of God
and gate of heaven, ~HAVE MERCY ON US.

Heart of Jesus, aflame with love
for us, ~HAVE MERCY ON US.

Heart of Jesus, source of justice
and love, ~HAVE MERCY ON US.

Heart of Jesus, full of goodness
and love, ~HAVE MERCY ON US.

Heart of Jesus, well-spring of
all virtue, ~HAVE MERCY ON US.

Heart of Jesus, worthy of all praise, ~HAVE MERCY ON US.

Heart of Jesus, king and center
of all hearts, ~HAVE MERCY ON US.

Heart of Jesus, treasure-house of
wisdom and knowledge, ~HAVE MERCY ON US.

Heart of Jesus, in whom there
dwells the fullness of God, ~HAVE MERCY ON US.

Heart of Jesus, in whom the Father
is well pleased, ~HAVE MERCY ON US.

Heart of Jesus, from whose fullness
we have all received, ~HAVE MERCY ON US.

Heart of Jesus, desire of the
eternal hills, ~HAVE MERCY ON US.

Heart of Jesus, patient and full
of mercy, ~HAVE MERCY ON US.

Heart of Jesus, generous to all who
turn to you, ~HAVE MERCY ON US.

Heart of Jesus, fountain of life
and holiness, ~HAVE MERCY ON US.

Heart of Jesus, atonement for our sins, ~HAVE MERCY ON US.
Heart of Jesus, overwhelmed
    with insults,   ~HAVE MERCY ON US.
Heart of Jesus, broken for our sins,   ~HAVE MERCY ON US.
Heart of Jesus, obedient even to death,   ~HAVE MERCY ON US.
Heart of Jesus, pierced by a lance,   ~HAVE MERCY ON US.
Heart of Jesus, source of all consolation, ~HAVE MERCY ON US.
Heart of Jesus, our life and resurrection, ~HAVE MERCY ON US.
Heart of Jesus, our peace
    and reconciliation,   ~HAVE MERCY ON US.
Heart of Jesus, victim for our sins,   ~HAVE MERCY ON US.
Heart of Jesus, salvation of all who
    trust in you,   ~HAVE MERCY ON US.
Heart of Jesus, hope of all who
    die in you,   ~HAVE MERCY ON US.
Heart of Jesus, delight of all the saints, ~HAVE MERCY ON US.

(Pause for spontaneous prayer.)

Lamb of God, you take away
    the sins of the world,   ~HAVE MERCY ON US.
Lamb of God, you take away
    the sins of the world,   ~HAVE MERCY ON US.
Lamb of God, you take away
    the sins of the world,   ~HAVE MERCY ON US.

Jesus, gentle and humble of heart.
~TOUCH OUR HEARTS AND MAKE THEM LIKE YOUR OWN.

Let us pray:

Father,
we rejoice in the gifts of love
we have received from the heart of Jesus your Son.
Open our hearts to share his life
and continue to bless us with his love.
We ask this in the name of Jesus the Lord.
~AMEN.[88]

Litany of the Precious Blood of Jesus

Lord, have mercy.   ~LORD, HAVE MERCY.
Christ, have mercy.   ~CHRIST, HAVE MERCY.
Lord, have mercy.   ~LORD, HAVE MERCY.

God our Father in heaven   ~HAVE MERCY ON US.
God the Son,
Redeemer of the world   ~HAVE MERCY ON US.
God the Holy Spirit   ~HAVE MERCY ON US.
Holy Trinity, one God   ~HAVE MERCY ON US.

Blood of Christ,
only Son of the Father,   ~BE OUR SALVATION.

Blood of Christ, incarnate Word,   ~BE OUR SALVATION.
Blood of Christ, of the new and
    eternal covenant,   ~BE OUR SALVATION.
Blood of Christ, that spilled
    to the ground,   ~BE OUR SALVATION.
Blood of Christ, that flowed
    at the scourging,   ~BE OUR SALVATION.
Blood of Christ, dripping from
    the thorns,   ~BE OUR SALVATION.
Blood of Christ, shed on the cross, ~BE OUR SALVATION.
Blood of Christ, the price of
    our redemption,   ~BE OUR SALVATION.
Blood of Christ, our only claim
    to pardon,   ~BE OUR SALVATION.
Blood of Christ, our blessing cup,   ~BE OUR SALVATION.
Blood of Christ, in which we
    are washed,   ~BE OUR SALVATION.
Blood of Christ, torrent of mercy,   ~BE OUR SALVATION.
Blood of Christ, that overcomes evil, ~BE OUR SALVATION.
Blood of Christ, strength of the martyrs, ~BE OUR SALVATION.
Blood of Christ, endurance of the saints, ~BE OUR SALVATION.

Blood of Christ, that makes the
barren fruitful,   ~BE OUR SALVATION.
Blood of Christ, protection of
the threatened,   ~BE OUR SALVATION.
Blood of Christ, comfort of the weary, ~BE OUR SALVATION.
Blood of Christ, solace of the mourner, ~BE OUR SALVATION.
Blood of Christ, hope of the repentant, ~BE OUR SALVATION.
Blood of Christ, consolation of
the dying,   ~BE OUR SALVATION.
Blood of Christ, our peace
and refreshment,   ~BE OUR SALVATION.
Blood of Christ, our pledge of life, ~BE OUR SALVATION.
Blood of Christ, by which we pass
to glory,   ~BE OUR SALVATION.
Blood of Christ, most worthy of honor, ~BE OUR SALVATION.

(Pause for spontaneous prayer.)

Lamb of God, you take away the
sins of the world   ~HAVE MERCY ON US.
Lamb of God, you take away the
sins of the world   ~HAVE MERCY ON US.
Lamb of God, you take away the
sins of the world   ~HAVE MERCY ON US.

Lord, you redeemed us by your blood.

~YOU HAVE MADE US A KINGDOM TO SERVE OUR GOD.

Let us pray:

Father,
by the blood of your Son
you have set us free and saved us from death.
Continue your work of love within us,
that by constantly celebrating the mystery of our salvation
we may reach the eternal life it promises.
We ask this through Christ our Lord.

~AMEN.[89]

Litany of the Blessed
Sacrament of the Altar

Lord, have mercy. ~LORD, HAVE MERCY.
Christ, have mercy. ~CHRIST, HAVE MERCY.
Lord, have mercy. ~LORD, HAVE MERCY.

God our Father in heaven, ~HAVE MERCY ON US.
God the Son, Redeemer of the world, ~HAVE MERCY ON US.
God the Holy Spirit, ~HAVE MERCY ON US.
Holy Trinity, one God, ~HAVE MERCY ON US.

Word made flesh and living
among us, ~CHRIST, HAVE MERCY ON US.

Pure and acceptable sacrifice,
Hidden manna from above,
Living bread that came down from heaven,
Bread of life for a hungry world,
Chalice of blessing,
Precious blood that washes away our sins,
Memorial of God's undying love,
Food that lasts for eternal life,
Mystery of faith,
Medicine of immortality,
Food of God's chosen,
Perpetual presence in our tabernacles,
Viaticum of those who die in the Lord,
Pledge of future glory,

Be merciful, ~SPARE US, GOOD LORD.
Be merciful, ~GRACIOUSLY HEAR US, GOOD LORD.

By the great longing you had to eat
the Passover with your disciples, ~GOOD LORD, DELIVER US.

By your humility in washing their feet,
By your loving gift of this divine sacrament,

By the five wounds of your precious body,
By your sacrificial death on the cross,
By the piercing of your sacred heart,
By your rising to new life,
By your gift of the Paraclete Spirit,
By your return in glory to judge the living and the dead,

(Pause for spontaneous prayer.)

Lamb of God, you take away the
   sins of the world, ~HAVE MERCY ON US.
Lamb of God, you take away the sins
   of the world, ~HAVE MERCY ON US.
Lamb of God, you take away the sins
   of the world, ~HAVE MERCY ON US.

You gave them bread from heaven to be their food.
~AND THIS BREAD CONTAINED ALL GOODNESS.

Let us pray:

Lord Jesus Christ,
you gave us the Eucharist
as the memorial of your suffering and death.
May our worship of this sacrament of your Body
   and Blood
help us to experience the salvation you won for us
and the peace of your kingdom,
where you live with the Father and the Holy Spirit,
one God forever and ever.
~AMEN.[90]

Litany of Our Lady (Loreto)

Lord, have mercy.	~LORD, HAVE MERCY.
Christ, have mercy.	~CHRIST, HAVE MERCY.
Lord, have mercy.	~LORD, HAVE MERCY.
God our Father in heaven,	~HAVE MERCY ON US.
God the Son, Redeemer of the world,	~HAVE MERCY ON US.
God the Holy Spirit,	~HAVE MERCY ON US.
Holy Trinity, one God,	~HAVE MERCY ON US.
Holy Mary,	~PRAY FOR US.
Holy Mother of God,	~PRAY FOR US.
Most honored of virgins,	~PRAY FOR US.
Mother of Christ,	~PRAY FOR US.
Mother of the Church,	~PRAY FOR US.
Mother of divine grace,	~PRAY FOR US.
Mother most pure,	~PRAY FOR US.
Mother of chaste love,	~PRAY FOR US.
Mother and virgin,	~PRAY FOR US.
Sinless Mother,	~PRAY FOR US.
Dearest of mothers,	~PRAY FOR US.
Model of motherhood,	~PRAY FOR US.
Mother of good counsel,	~PRAY FOR US.
Mother of our Creator,	~PRAY FOR US.
Mother of our Savior,	~PRAY FOR US.
Virgin most wise,	~PRAY FOR US.
Virgin rightly praised,	~PRAY FOR US.
Virgin rightly renowned,	~PRAY FOR US.
Virgin most powerful,	~PRAY FOR US.
Virgin gentle in mercy,	~PRAY FOR US.
Faithful virgin,	~PRAY FOR US.
Mirror of justice,	~PRAY FOR US.
Throne of wisdom,	~PRAY FOR US.
Cause of our joy,	~PRAY FOR US.

Shrine of the Spirit,	~PRAY FOR US.
Glory of Israel,	~PRAY FOR US.
Vessel of selfless devotion,	~PRAY FOR US.
Mystical rose,	~PRAY FOR US.
Tower of David,	~PRAY FOR US.
Tower of ivory,	~PRAY FOR US.
House of gold,	~PRAY FOR US.
Ark of the Covenant,	~PRAY FOR US.
Gate of heaven,	~PRAY FOR US.
Morning star,	~PRAY FOR US.
Health of the sick,	~PRAY FOR US.
Refuge of sinners,	~PRAY FOR US.
Comfort of the troubled,	~PRAY FOR US.
Help of Christians,	~PRAY FOR US.
Queen of angels,	~PRAY FOR US.
Queen of patriarchs and prophets,	~PRAY FOR US.
Queen of apostles and martyrs,	~PRAY FOR US.
Queen of confessors and virgins,	~PRAY FOR US.
Queen of all saints,	~PRAY FOR US.
Queen conceived in grace,	~PRAY FOR US.
Queen raised up to glory,	~PRAY FOR US.
Queen of the rosary,	~PRAY FOR US.
Queen of peace,	~PRAY FOR US.

(Pause for spontaneous prayer.)

Lamb of God, you take away the sins of the world,	~HAVE MERCY ON US.
Lamb of God, you take away the sins of the world,	~HAVE MERCY ON US.
Lamb of God, you take away the sins of the world,	~HAVE MERCY ON US.

Pray for us, holy Mother of God.
~THAT WE MAY BECOME WORTHY OF THE PROMISES OF CHRIST.

Let us pray:

Eternal God,
let your people enjoy constant health in mind and body.
Through the intercession of the Virgin Mary
free us from the sorrows of this life
and lead us to happiness in the life to come.
Grant this through Christ our Lord.

~AMEN.[91]

Litany of the Blessed Virgin Mary

Lord, have mercy.   ~LORD, HAVE MERCY.
Christ, have mercy.   ~CHRIST, HAVE MERCY.
Lord, have mercy.   ~LORD, HAVE MERCY.

God our Father in heaven,   ~HAVE MERCY ON US.
God the Son, Redeemer of the world,   ~HAVE MERCY ON US.
God the Holy Spirit,   ~HAVE MERCY ON US.
Holy Trinity, one God,   ~HAVE MERCY ON US.

Holy Mary,   ~PRAY FOR US.
Holy Mother of God,   ~PRAY FOR US.
Most honored of virgins,   ~PRAY FOR US.

Chosen daughter of the Father,   ~PRAY FOR US.
Mother of Christ the King,   ~PRAY FOR US.
Glory of the Holy Spirit,   ~PRAY FOR US.

Virgin daughter of Zion,   ~PRAY FOR US.
Virgin poor and humble,   ~PRAY FOR US.
Virgin gentle and obedient,   ~PRAY FOR US.

Handmaid of the Lord,   ~PRAY FOR US.
Mother of the Lord,   ~PRAY FOR US.
Helper of the Redeemer,   ~PRAY FOR US.

Full of grace,	~PRAY FOR US.
Fountain of beauty,	~PRAY FOR US.
Model of virtue,	~PRAY FOR US.
Finest fruit of the redemption,	~PRAY FOR US.
Perfect disciple of Christ,	~PRAY FOR US.
Untarnished image of the Church,	~PRAY FOR US.
Woman transformed,	~PRAY FOR US.
Woman clothed with the sun,	~PRAY FOR US.
Woman crowned with stars,	~PRAY FOR US.
Gentle lady,	~PRAY FOR US.
Gracious lady,	~PRAY FOR US.
Our Lady,	~PRAY FOR US.
Joy of Israel,	~PRAY FOR US.
Splendor of the Church,	~PRAY FOR US.
Pride of the human race,	~PRAY FOR US.
Advocate of peace,	~PRAY FOR US.
Minister of holiness,	~PRAY FOR US.
Champion of God's people,	~PRAY FOR US.
Queen of love,	~PRAY FOR US.
Queen of mercy,	~PRAY FOR US.
Queen of peace,	~PRAY FOR US.
Queen of angels,	~PRAY FOR US.
Queen of patriarchs and prophets,	~PRAY FOR US.
Queen of apostles and martyrs,	~PRAY FOR US.
Queen of confessors and virgins,	~PRAY FOR US.
Queen of all saints,	~PRAY FOR US.
Queen conceived without original sin,	~PRAY FOR US.
Queen assumed into heaven,	~PRAY FOR US.
Queen of all the earth,	~PRAY FOR US.
Queen of heaven,	~PRAY FOR US.
Queen of the universe,	~PRAY FOR US.

(Pause for spontaneous prayer.)

Lamb of God, you take away
   the sins of the world,   ~SPARE US, O LORD.
Lamb of God, you take away
   the sins of the world,   ~HEAR US, O LORD.
Lamb of God, you take away
   the sins of the world,   ~HAVE MERCY ON US.

Pray for us, O glorious Mother of the Lord.
~THAT WE MAY BECOME WORTHY OF THE PROMISES OF CHRIST.

Let us pray:

God of mercy,
listen to the prayers of your servants
who have honored your handmaid Mary as mother
   and queen.
Grant that by your grace
we may serve you and our neighbor on earth
and be welcomed into your eternal kingdom.

We ask this through Christ our Lord.

~AMEN.[92]

The Rosary of the Blessed Virgin Mary

Of all the popular devotions beloved of Catholics, the rosary best illustrates "the inventive genius of medieval piety in the West" and presents "a balanced fullness known to no other practice of private devotion."[93] Surely that is why saints and mystics, bishops and popes, popular preachers and theologians—and in a special way Mary herself—have expressed delight in this form of prayer and have promoted it so widely.

The origins of the rosary lie in the Marian piety of the Christian Middle Ages. In private devotion the whole Psalter of 150 psalms was divided into three groups of fifty psalms each. In imitation of this way of praying the psalms, there grew up a variety of popular devotions made up of 50 or 150 Our Fathers or Hail Marys that were often counted on knotted strings or beads. These were psalters of praise in honor of Jesus or Mary, and a psalter of Mary was often called a "rosary" (a gift of roses), a chaplet, a wreath, or a bouquet.

Around 1365 a devout Carthusian monk arranged 150 Hail Marys into groups of ten (decades) and put an Our Father between each decade. Around 1409, another Carthusian, Dominic of Prussia, composed a pamphlet that attached fifty thoughts about the lives of Jesus and Mary to a rosary of fifty Hail Marys. Soon this form of rosary was also divided into decades, with an Our Father between each decade.

The blood brother of Dominic of Prussia was a member of the Order of Preachers, and inspired by his brother's devotion, he introduced this rosary to his Dominican confreres. Soon this devotion that grew up in the silence of the cloister was preached far and wide in and outside of Dominican houses all over Europe.

To keep all these thoughts before one's mind required a booklet, and so the expression to "read the rosary." With the spread of printing and wood engraving, rosary booklets became common, but since it was too expensive to engrave and print 150 illustrations, the rosary was reduced to fifteen mysteries and fifteen pictures, one for each decade. With the passage of time, the rosary of 150 read mysteries tended to die out, but the fifteen-decade rosary endured, often accompanied by fifteen pictures—for example, for the first mystery, the angel saluting Mary and announcing the coming of the Messiah.

But then, since the meditative aspect of the rosary was felt to be slipping into the background, various narrative meditations were introduced before each decade to inform and concentrate the mind. One of the best known of these meditations was composed by the renowned Marian apostle St. Louis de Montfort around 1700.

The rosary presented here draws on this historical background and on the fresh initiatives of Pope John Paul II (*Rosarium Virginis Mariae,* October 16, 2002), and proposes several helpful ways of praying it.

The backbone or skeleton of the full rosary is now made up of twenty Our Fathers, two hundred Hail Marys, and twenty Glory to the Fathers. These vocal prayers are divided into twenty decades, and each one is composed of one Our Father, ten Hail Marys, and one Glory to the Father in honor of each mystery.

The flesh and blood of the rosary is made up of the twenty events or mysteries of the life of our Lord and our Lady that we meditate upon while reciting the vocal prayers.

The soul of the rosary is the Holy Spirit, who inspired the founders of this remarkable devotion and who inspires and assists each believing Christian who prays it devoutly and frequently.

At the advice of Pope John Paul II, those who say five decades a day will usually pray the five Joyful Mysteries on Monday and Saturday, the five Luminous Mysteries on Thursday, the five sorrowful Mysteries on Tuesday and Friday, and the five Glorious Mysteries on Wednesday and Sunday. In adding the five Mysteries of Light (Luminous Mysteries) to the traditional three sets, the pope has also recommended a period of meditative silence after the announcement of each mystery and a suitable collect prayer at the end of each decade. He also suggests the use of icons to focus attention on each mystery, a return to the purpose of the wood engravings of the sixteenth century.

Ways of Praying the Rosary

The *first and most basic* way to pray the rosary is to announce each of the twenty mysteries in turn and then to recite the vocal prayers of each decade slowly and carefully in honor of that mystery. The mind is focused in a general way on the mystery, but the concentration is more on each vocal prayer as it is said.

A *second* way is to announce the mystery and then read one of the suggested Bible passages to inform and sustain the meditation. A period of silence is

The Rosary of the Blessed Virgin Mary **229**

recommended before beginning the vocal prayers, and an appropriate prayer is supplied for the end of each decade. One might also consider saying only one or two decades at a time and put more effort, at first, into meditating on the biblical event directly. This is a particularly helpful way for those without much familiarity with Holy Scripture; they would do well to take this second step as soon as they have mastered the mechanics of the first way.

A *third* way is to set aside these longer passages of Scripture and use only one short quotation to help begin and center meditation; for example, for the first mystery: "The Word was made flesh, and dwelt among us" (John 1:14).

A *fourth* way is to attach an appropriate phrase or clause to the first half of the Hail Mary after the word *Jesus:*

Hail, Mary, . . . and blessed is the fruit of your womb, Jesus,

who was conceived at the message of an angel.

~HOLY MARY, MOTHER OF GOD, . . . AMEN.

Such phrases are provided below, but experienced users of the rosary might like to select or compose their own. The use of such clauses is considered "a praiseworthy custom" by Pope John Paul II.

A *fifth* way—for group prayer—is to announce the mystery and invite members of the group to take turns making a short meditation out loud before the group takes up the vocal prayers of each decade.

A *sixth* way is to use the beads as a kind of counter and say over and over again the key words of the Hail Mary: *Jesus* or *Mary;* the longer form of the Jesus Prayer: "Lord Jesus Christ, Son of the living

God, have mercy on me, a sinner"; or some favorite phrase from Scripture.

Whatever the method, the main thing to remember is that the physical handling of the beads, the constant repetition of the familiar vocal prayers, and the inner sense of the life-giving mysteries are conducive to the deepest forms of Christian prayer. The rosary is one of the finest methods ever discovered to enshrine in prayer the central themes of the gospel.

The Joyful Mysteries

1. The Angel Gabriel Brings the Good News to Mary

Bible Readings: Isaiah 7:10–15; Luke 1:26–38

Key Phrase: "Now all this happened in order to make come true what the Lord had said through the prophet, 'A virgin will become pregnant and have a son, and he will be called Immanuel'" (Matthew 1:22–23 TEV).

Hail, Mary, . . . blessed is the fruit of your womb, Jesus,
  who was conceived at the message of an angel.
  ~HOLY MARY, MOTHER OF GOD, PRAY FOR
    US SINNERS . . .

PRAYER AT THE END OF THE DECADE:
Pour forth, O Lord, your grace into our hearts
that we, to whom the incarnation of Christ
  your Son

was made known by the message of an angel,
may by his passion and cross
be brought to the glory of his resurrection;
through the same Christ our Lord.
~AMEN.

2. Mary Visits Her Cousin Elizabeth

Bible Readings: Jeremiah 1:4–10; Luke 1:39–56

Key Phrase: "You will give birth to a son, and you will name him Jesus" (Luke 1:31 TEV).

Hail, Mary, . . . blessed is the fruit of your womb,
    Jesus,
    who consecrated the Baptist in the womb
        of his mother.
    ~HOLY MARY, MOTHER OF GOD, PRAY FOR
        US SINNERS . . .

PRAYER
God of your chosen people,
you inspired the Virgin Mary
to visit her cousin Elizabeth
and to sanctify the Baptist in her womb.
May the childbearing of Mary,
the beginning of our salvation,
enlighten and inspire us
to love God with all our heart
and serve our neighbor as ourselves.
We ask this through Christ our Lord.
~AMEN.

3. Jesus' Birth in Bethlehem of Judea

Bible Readings: Micah 5:1–5; Matthew 2:1–12;
Luke 2:1–20; Galatians 4:1–7

Key Phrase: "I am here with good news for you,
which will bring great joy to all the people"
(Luke 2:10 TEV).

Hail, Mary, . . . blessed is the fruit of your womb,
Jesus,
who was born for us in the stable of Bethlehem.
~HOLY MARY, MOTHER OF GOD, PRAY FOR
US SINNERS . . .

PRAYER
Abba, dear Father,
by the fruitful virginity of Blessed Mary
you conferred the benefits of eternal salvation
on the whole human race.
May we experience the power of her intercession
through whom we received the Author of life,
Jesus Christ our Lord, who lives and reigns
with you
and the Holy Spirit, one God, forever and ever.
~AMEN.

4. Jesus Meets Old Simeon and Anna in the Temple

Bible Readings: Luke 2:22–38; Hebrews 9:6–14

Key Phrase: "With my own eyes I have seen your
salvation, which you have prepared in the presence of all peoples" (Luke 2:30–31 TEV).

Hail, Mary, . . . blessed is the fruit of your womb,
Jesus,
the glory of your people Israel.
~HOLY MARY, MOTHER OF GOD, PRAY FOR
US SINNERS . . .

PRAYER

Almighty and everlasting God,
old Simeon and Anna the prophet
rejoiced at the coming of your Son
into the temple of Jerusalem.
May we share their joy
and await your coming in glory
at the end of time.
We ask this through Christ our Lord.
~AMEN.

5. The Boy Jesus in the Temple

Bible Readings: Luke 2:41–50; John 12:44–50;
1 Corinthians 2:6–16

Key Phrase: "Didn't you know that I had to be in
my Father's house?" (Luke 2:49 TEV).

Hail, Mary, . . . blessed is the fruit of your womb,
Jesus,
the power and the wisdom of God.
~HOLY MARY, MOTHER OF GOD, PRAY FOR
US SINNERS . . .

PRAYER

Wise and merciful God,
you drew your dear Son into the circle
of the teachers of the Law,
listening to them and asking them questions.
With Mary and Joseph
may we find Jesus in the Father's house
and return with him to the obscurity
of the hidden years at Nazareth
as he prepares for his public life and mission.
We ask this through the same Christ our Lord.
~Amen.

After the Joyful Mysteries: *Alma Redemptoris Mater*

Mother of Christ, our hope, our patroness,
Star of the sea, our beacon in distress.
Guide to the shores of everlasting day
God's holy people on their pilgrim way.

Virgin, in you God made his dwelling place;
Mother of all the living, full of grace,
blessed are you: God's word you did believe;
"yes" on your lips undid the "no" of Eve.

Daughter of God, who bore his holy One,
dearest of all to Christ, your loving Son,
show us his face, O Mother, as on earth,
loving us all, you gave our Savior birth.[94]

Pray for us, holy Mother of God,
~That we may become worthy of the promises
   of Christ.

Let us pray:

Abba, dear Father,
in your plan for our salvation
your Word was made flesh,
announced by an angel
and born of the Virgin Mary.
May we who believe that she is
    the Mother of God
receive the help of her prayers.
We ask this through Christ our Lord.
~AMEN.

The Luminous Mysteries

1. Jesus Is Baptized by John in the Jordan

Bible Readings: Mark 1:9–11; Matthew 3:13–17;
Luke 3:21–22; John 1:29–34

Key Phrase: "You are my own dear Son. I am
pleased with you" (Mark 1:11 TEV).

Hail, Mary, . . . blessed is the fruit of your womb,
    Jesus,
    who was baptized by John in the Jordan.
    ~HOLY MARY, MOTHER OF GOD, PRAY FOR
    US SINNERS . . .

PRAYER AT THE END OF THE DECADE:
Almighty and everlasting God,
you revealed your own dear Son to us
when the Spirit came down like a dove from heaven

and rested on him as he emerged from Jordan's
   waters.
May we who are reborn of water and the Holy
   Spirit
remain in truth your beloved children,
faithful witnesses to your power and glory.
We ask this through Christ our Lord.
~AMEN.

2. Jesus at the Wedding Feast of Cana

Bible Readings: John 2:1–11

Key Phrase: "There Jesus revealed his glory, and
his disciples believed in him" (John 2:11 TEV).

Hail, Mary, . . . blessed is the fruit of your womb,
   Jesus,
   *who revealed his glory at the wedding feast
   of Cana.*
   ~HOLY MARY, MOTHER OF GOD, PRAY FOR
      US SINNERS . . .

PRAYER

Abba, dear Father,
your beloved Son Jesus revealed his glory
at the wedding feast of Cana,
where his first disciples believed in him.
By the intercession of Mary his Mother,
help us to admire Jesus in his signs and wonders
and to follow his teaching as devoted disciples.
We ask this through the same Christ our Lord.
~AMEN.

3. The Reign of God Is at Hand

Bible Readings: Mark 1:14–15; Matthew 4:12–17; Luke 4:14–15

Key Phrase: "The right time has come, and the Kingdom of God is near!" (Mark 1:15 TEV)

Hail, Mary, . . . blessed is the fruit of your womb, Jesus,
  who proclaimed the arrival of God's reign.
  ~HOLY MARY, MOTHER OF GOD, PRAY FOR
    US SINNERS . . .

PRAYER

Abba, dear Father,
you sent your only Son to proclaim your reign
in heaven and on earth.
By the words and deeds of Jesus,
establish your reign in our hearts and minds
and help us make peace throughout the world.
We ask this through the same Christ our Lord.
~AMEN.

4. Jesus Is Transfigured on Mount Tabor

Bible Readings: Mark 9:2–9; Matthew 17:1–9; Luke 9:28–36

Key Phrase: "This is my Son, whom I have chosen—listen to him!" (Luke 9:35 TEV).

Hail, Mary, . . . blessed is the fruit of your womb, Jesus,
  *who appeared to his chosen disciples on
    Mount Tabor.*

~HOLY MARY, MOTHER OF GOD, PRAY FOR
US SINNERS . . .

PRAYER
God of might and majesty,
in the glorious transfiguration of your dear Son,
by the testimony of the prophets Moses and Elijah,
you confirmed the mystery of his being
and by your voice from the bright cloud
foreshadowed our wonderful adoption as your
children.
In your loving-kindness
make us coheirs with the King of glory,
who lives and reigns with you and the Holy Spirit,
one God, forever and ever.
~AMEN.

5. The Lord's Supper
Bible Readings: Mark 14:22–26; Matthew
26:26–30; Luke 22:14–20; 1 Corinthians 11:23–25

Key Phrase: "This is my blood which seals God's
covenant" (Mark 14:24 TEV).

Hail, Mary, . . . blessed is the fruit of your womb,
Jesus,
*who established God's new covenant, sealed
with his blood.*
~HOLY MARY, MOTHER OF GOD, PRAY FOR
US SINNERS . . .

PRAYER

Redeemer of the world,
in this wonderful Sacrament of the altar,
you left us a gracious memorial
of your blessed passion, death, and resurrection.
May we reverence the sacred mysteries
   of your body and blood
and be always attentive to these precious gifts
of your lasting presence among us.
You live and reign, now and forever.
~Amen.

After the Mysteries of Light: *Sub tuum praesidium*

We turn to you for protection,
~holy Mother of God.
Listen to our prayers
and help us in our needs.
Save us from every danger
glorious and blessed Virgin.[95]

Pray for us, holy Mother of God.
~That we may become worthy of the promises
   of Christ.

Let us pray:

Father of holiness,
for the journey of your pilgrim church on earth,
you have provided the Virgin Mary as a sign and
   beacon.
Through her intercession

sustain our faith and enliven our hope,
that no obstacle may divert us
from the road that brings us salvation.
Please grant this through Christ our Lord.
~AMEN.[96]

The Sorrowful Mysteries

1. The Agony of Jesus in the Garden of Gethsemane

Bible Readings: Matthew 26:36–46; Mark 14:26–42; Luke 22:39–53; John 18:1–12

Key Phrase: "In great anguish Jesus prayed even more fervently; his sweat was like drops of blood falling to the ground" (Luke 22:44 TEV).

Hail, Mary, . . . blessed is the fruit of your womb, Jesus,
who prayed in great anguish to his Father.
~HOLY MARY, MOTHER OF GOD, PRAY FOR
US SINNERS . . .

PRAYER AT THE END OF THE DECADE:
Savior of the world,
by your agony in the Garden of Gethsemane,
as you foresaw how your disciples would desert
you, Judas betray you, and Peter deny you,
grant us the grace to watch and pray
for strength and courage in the hour of trial
that we may remain faithful to the end.
You live and reign, now and forever.
~AMEN.

2. Jesus Is Scourged at Pilate's Orders

Bible Readings: Isaiah 50:5–9; Matthew 27:15–26;
Mark 15:6–15; Luke 23:13–25; John 18:38–19:1

Key Phrase: "After Pilate had Jesus whipped,
he handed him over to be crucified"
(Matthew 27:26 TEV).

Hail, Mary, . . . blessed is the fruit of your womb,
   Jesus,
   who was bruised for our offenses.
      ~HOLY MARY, MOTHER OF GOD, PRAY FOR
         US SINNERS . . .

PRAYER
Loving Father,
your innocent Son was betrayed
into the hands of the wicked
and judged worthy of death.
By the blood that flowed from his lacerated body,
may we worship him in the mystery of suffering
and see him in the tortured victims
of brutal judicial systems of our own time.
In Jesus' name, we ask it.
~AMEN.

3. Jesus Is Crowned with Thorns, Mocked, and Slapped

Bible Readings: Matthew 27:27–31; Mark
15:16–20; John 19:1–5

Key Phrase: "[The soldiers] made a crown out of
thorny branches and placed it on his head . . . ;

then they knelt before him and made fun of him"
(Matthew 27:29 TEV).

Hail, Mary, . . . blessed is the fruit of your
  womb, Jesus,
  a man of sorrows and acquainted with grief.
  ~HOLY MARY, MOTHER OF GOD, PRAY FOR
    US SINNERS . . .

PRAYER
Gracious God,
after Pilate handed Jesus over to be crucified
the whole Roman cohort gathered around him
to make him a mock king with a crown of thorns,
a purple robe, and scepter of reed.
By the mockery, the ridicule, and the slapping,
help us to overcome our pride and insolence
and become worthy disciples of him
who took the form of a slave
and humbled himself even to the point of death.
In the name of Jesus, we ask it.
  ~AMEN.

4. Jesus Walks the Way of the Cross
Bible Readings: Mark 8:31–38; 15:21–28; Luke
23:26–32; John 19:16–22; Philippians 2:6–11

Key Phrase: "Jesus said, 'Women of Jerusalem!
Don't cry for me, but for yourselves and your
children'" (Luke 23:28 TEV).

Hail, Mary, . . . blessed is the fruit of your womb,
  Jesus,

who was crushed for our sins.
  ~HOLY MARY, MOTHER OF GOD, PRAY FOR
    US SINNERS . . .

PRAYER
Lord Jesus, Word of God,
as you walked the bitter way of the cross,
compassionate women wept and wailed
at the sight of your suffering,
but you insisted for our sake
that compassion leading to repentance
was more needed than pity for your pains.
As we contemplate your passion and death,
give us heartfelt sorrow for our sins,
and reward us with the purging gift of tears.
In your blessed name we ask it.
  ~AMEN.

5. Jesus Is Crucified and Dies on the Cross
Bible Readings: Mark 15:33–39; John 19:17–37;
Hebrews 9:11–14; Acts 2:22–24

Key Phrase: "Father! In your hands I place my
spirit" (Luke 23:46 TEV).

Hail, Mary, . . . blessed is the fruit of your womb,
    Jesus,
    by whose wounds we are healed.
  ~HOLY MARY, MOTHER OF GOD, PRAY FOR
    US SINNERS . . .

PRAYER

Lord Jesus Christ,
in your agony and bitter death,
you surrendered your spirit to your Father
and descended among the imprisoned spirits
to enlighten and release them.
Continue, in your mercy,
to break open the gates of death and hell
and to bring us at last to the resurrection of
the body
and life everlasting in the world to come,
where you live and reign with the Father and the
Holy Spirit,
one God, forever and ever.
~AMEN.

After the Sorrowful Mysteries:
Salve, Regina

Hail, holy Queen, Mother of mercy,
~HAIL, OUR LIFE, OUR SWEETNESS, AND OUR HOPE.
TO YOU WE CRY, THE CHILDREN OF EVE;
TO YOU WE SEND UP OUR SIGHS,
MOURNING AND WEEPING IN THIS LAND OF EXILE.
TURN, THEN, MOST GRACIOUS ADVOCATE,
YOUR EYES OF MERCY TOWARD US;
LEAD US HOME AT LAST
AND SHOW US THE BLESSED FRUIT OF YOUR WOMB,
JESUS:
O CLEMENT, O LOVING, O SWEET VIRGIN MARY.[97]

Mother of Sorrows, pray for us.

~THAT WE MAY BECOME WORTHY OF THE PROMISES
   OF CHRIST.

Let us pray:
Abba, dear Father,
as your Son hung on the cross,
his Mother Mary stood by him,
sharing his sufferings.
May your Church be united with Christ
in his suffering and death
and so come to share in his rising
   to new life,
where he lives and reigns with you
and the Holy Spirit,
one God, forever and ever.
~AMEN.

The Glorious Mysteries
1. God Raises Christ from the Grave
Bible Readings: Mark 16:1–8; Matthew 28:1–10;
Luke 24:1–11; John 20:1–10; 1 Corinthians
15:1–11; Romans 6:1–14

Key Phrase: "Was it not necessary for the Messiah
to suffer these things and then to enter his glory?"
(Luke 24:26 TEV).

Hail, Mary, . . . blessed is the fruit of your womb,
   Jesus,
   who died for our sins and rose for our justification.
   ~HOLY MARY, MOTHER OF GOD, PRAY FOR
      US SINNERS . . .

PRAYER AT THE END OF THE DECADE:
Risen Lord and Savior,
we rejoice in the power of your holy resurrection!
As we prepare for your coming again in majesty,
cleanse us from all our sins,
make us grow into your image and likeness,
and fill us with joy of our baptism,
by which we are the true children of God.
You live and reign, now and forever.
~AMEN.

2. Christ Ascends into Heaven

Bible Readings: Matthew 28:16–20; Luke 24:44–53; Acts 1:1–11; Ephesians 2:4–7

Key Phrase: "Jesus was taken up to heaven as they watched him, and a cloud hid him from their sight" (Acts 1:9 TEV).

Hail, Mary, . . . blessed is the fruit of your womb, Jesus,
who now sits at the right hand of the Father.
~HOLY MARY, MOTHER OF GOD, PRAY FOR
US SINNERS . . .

PRAYER
God our Father,
make us joyful in the ascension
of your Son Jesus Christ.
May we follow him into the new creation,
for his ascension is our glory and our hope.
We ask this through Christ our Lord.
~AMEN.

3. Pentecost: The Gift of the Spirit

Bible Readings: John 14:15–21; Acts 2:1–11; Acts 4:23–31; Acts 10:44–48

Key Phrase: "I myself will send upon you what my Father has promised" (Luke 24:49 TEV).

Hail, Mary, . . . blessed is the fruit of your womb, Jesus,
> *who sends us the Holy Spirit as he promised.*
> ~HOLY MARY, MOTHER OF GOD, PRAY FOR US SINNERS . . .

PRAYER

Heavenly King, Consoler, Spirit of Truth,
present in all places and filling all things,
treasury of blessings and giver of life:
Come and dwell in us.
Cleanse us from every trace of sin,
and save our souls,
O gracious Lord.
~AMEN.

4. The Falling Asleep and Assumption of Mary

Bible Readings: John 11:17–27; 1 Corinthians 15:12–57; Revelations 21:1–6

Key Phrase: "Thanks be to God who gives us the victory through our Lord Jesus Christ!" (1 Corinthians 15:57 TEV).

Hail, Mary, . . . blessed is the fruit of your womb, Jesus,

who makes all things new.

~HOLY MARY, MOTHER OF GOD, PRAY FOR
US SINNERS . . .

PRAYER

Father in heaven,
all creation rightly gives you praise
for all life and holiness come from you.
In the plan of your wisdom
she who bore Christ in her womb
was raised body and soul to glory
to be with him in heaven.
May we follow her example
in reflecting your holiness
and join with her hymn of endless praise.
We ask this through Christ our Lord.

~AMEN.

5. The Coronation of Mary and the Glory of All the Saints

Bible Readings: Matthew 5:1–12; Revelation 7:1–4, 9–12; Revelation 21:1–6

Key Phrase: "Happy are those whose greatest desire is to do what God requires" (Matthew 5:6 TEV).

Hail, Mary, . . . blessed is the fruit of your womb, Jesus,
who will come again in glory with all his saints.

~HOLY MARY, MOTHER OF GOD, PRAY FOR
US SINNERS . . .

PRAYER

Heavenly Father,
by the intercession of Mary our Queen
and of the whole company of heaven,
prepare your Church for the second coming
of our Lord, God, and Savior Jesus Christ,
who lives and reigns with you and the Holy Spirit,
now and forever.
~AMEN.

After the Glorious Mysteries: *Regina coeli*

Rejoice, O Queen of Heaven, alleluia!
FOR THE SON YOU BORE, ALLELUIA!
HAS ARISEN AS HE PROMISED, ALLELUIA!
PRAY FOR US TO GOD THE FATHER, ALLELUIA!

Rejoice and be glad, O Virgin Mary, alleluia!
~FOR THE LORD HAS TRULY RISEN, ALLELUIA!

Let us pray:

Abba, dear Father,
you give joy to the world
by the resurrection of your Son,
our Lord Jesus Christ.
Through the prayers of his Mother,
the Virgin Mary,
bring us to the happiness of eternal life.
We ask this through Christ our Lord.
~AMEN.

A Biblical Way of the Cross

Since the first pilgrims journeyed to the Holy Land to retrace in prayer our Lord's steps, they have wanted to walk his path from the court of Pontius Pilate to the hill of Golgotha and to the tomb that sheltered his dead body. To accommodate them, a series of stations—stopping points for meditation and prayer—were arranged in the city and in the Basilica of the Resurrection. In a variety of forms these stations were imitated in the home countries of the pilgrims and were ultimately arranged in the form of fourteen "stations of the cross." Some were derived directly from the Gospels, while others were the product of pious imagination. The Way of the Cross that is presented here is based solely on the events recorded in the four Gospels.

In a public celebration of the Way of the Cross in church, in chapel, or at an out-of-doors shrine, it is customary to move from station to station while meditating on the Passion. This is also done by individuals in church or chapel. At home, in private use, we may meditate on the Passion before a crucifix, using the following or similar texts from the Bible. This approach is especially recommended for those confined to their homes and beds.

First Station

Pilate Condemns Jesus to the Cross

LEADER: We adore you, O Christ, and we bless you,

ALL: ~FOR BY YOUR HOLY CROSS YOU HAVE REDEEMED THE WORLD.

READING   **MARK 15:1, 15–20** [98]

Early in the morning the chief priests met hurriedly with the elders, the teachers of the Law, and the whole Council, and made their plans. They put Jesus in chains, led him away, and handed him over to Pilate. Pilate wanted to please the crowd, so he set Barabbas free for them. Then he had Jesus whipped and handed him over to be crucified. The soldiers took Jesus inside the courtyard of the governor's palace. They put a purple robe on Jesus, made a crown of thorny branches, and put it on his head. Then they began to salute him: "Long live the King of the Jews!" They beat him over the head with a stick, spat on him, fell on their knees, and bowed down to him. When they had finished making fun of him, they took off the purple robe and put his own clothes back on him. Then they led him out to crucify him.

(Pause for meditation.)

LEADER: He was a man of sorrows

ALL: ~AND ACQUAINTED WITH GRIEF (ISAIAH 53:3).

PRAYER

Good Lord and Redeemer,
as Pontius Pilate washed his hands of you
and delivered you over to torture, contempt, and
　　mockery,
you refused to answer a word to your accusers.
By your patient silence,
help us to walk the way of the cross with you
as we adore your bloodstained footprints,
O Savior of the world,
now reigning from the tree of the cross.

ALL: ~AMEN.

Second Station

Simon of Cyrene Helps Jesus Carry His Cross

We adore you, O Christ, and we bless you.

~FOR BY YOUR HOLY CROSS YOU HAVE REDEEMED
　　THE WORLD.

READING　　　　　　　　**JOHN 19:17; MARK 15:21**

Jesus went out, carrying his cross, and came to
"The Place of the Skull," as it is called. (In
Hebrew it is called "Golgotha.") On the way they
met a man named Simon, who was coming into
the city from the country, and the soldiers forced
him to carry Jesus' cross.

(Pause for meditation.)

Bear one another's burdens,
~AND IN THIS WAY FULFILL THE LAW OF CHRIST
(GALATIANS 6:2).

PRAYER
Lord Jesus, falling under the weight of the cross,
you accepted the assistance of Simon
and with his help staggered on towards Golgotha.
By your weakness and your pain,
give us the courage and strength
to bear the crosses of our own lives
and to accept with gratitude
the help of those who come to our assistance.
~AMEN.

Third Station
The Weeping Women of Jerusalem
We adore you, O Christ and we bless you.
~FOR BY YOUR HOLY CROSS YOU HAVE REDEEMED
THE WORLD.

READING   **LUKE 23:27–31**
A large crowd of people followed Jesus; among
them were some women who were weeping and
wailing for him. Jesus turned to them and said,
"Women of Jerusalem! Don't cry for me, but for
yourselves and your children. For the days are
coming when people will say, 'How lucky are the
women who never had children, who never bore

babies, who never nursed them!' That will be the time when people will say to the mountains, 'Fall on us!' and to the hills, 'Hide us!' For if such things as these are done when the wood is green, what will happen when it is dry?"

(Pause for meditation.)

No one has greater love than this,
~To lay down one's life for one's friends
   (John 15:13).

Prayer
Lord Jesus, Word of God,
as you walked the bitter way of the cross,
compassionate women wept and wailed
at the sight of your suffering,
but you insisted for our sake
that compassion leading to repentance
was more needed than pity for your pains.
As we contemplate your passion and death,
give us heartfelt sorrow for our sins
and reward us with the purging gift of tears.
~Amen.

Fourth Station
Jesus Is Nailed to the Cross
We adore you, O Christ, and we bless you.
~For by your holy cross you have redeemed
   the world.

The soldiers took Jesus to a place called Golgotha, which means "The Place of the Skull." There they tried to give him wine mixed with a drug called myrrh, but Jesus would not drink it. It was nine o'clock in the morning when they crucified him. The notice of accusation against him said: "The King of the Jews." They also crucified two bandits with Jesus, one on his right and the other on his left. Jesus said, "Forgive them, Father! They don't know what they are doing."

(Pause for meditation.)

They tear holes in my hands and my feet,
~AND LAY ME IN THE DUST OF DEATH
(PSALM 22:16–17).

PRAYER
Lord Jesus, suffering servant of God,
at midmorning you were led to Golgotha
and nailed to the cross of pain
for the salvation of the world:
As we contemplate with love and pity
your five precious wounds,
fix deep in our hearts the words of David the
    prophet:
"They have pierced my hands and my feet,
I can count all my bones."
~AMEN.

Fifth Station
Jesus Is Deprived of His Clothing

We adore you, O Christ, and we bless you,

~For by your holy cross you have redeemed
the world.

Reading   **Psalm 22:18; John 19:23–24**

After the soldiers had crucified Jesus, they took
his clothes and divided them into four parts, one
for each soldier. They also took the robe, which
was made of one piece of woven cloth without
any seam in it. The soldiers said to one another,
"Let's not tear it; let's throw dice to see who will
get it." This happened in order to make the scripture come true: "They divided my clothes among
themselves and gambled for my robe." And this is
what the soldiers did.

(Pause for meditation.)

I am a worm, hardly human,

~Despised by all, mocked by the crowd
(Psalm 22:6).

Prayer

Jesus, humble servant of God,
you emptied yourself of your divine status
and assumed the nature of a slave;
even more, you became obedient unto death,
even death on a cross.

By the humiliation of your public crucifixion,
when soldiers divided your clothes among
    themselves
and threw dice for your seamless robe,
be the salvation of our humble condition
and help us endure in patience
until all is accomplished.
~AMEN.

Sixth Station

Jesus Is Mocked and Derided

We adore you, O Christ, and we bless you,
~FOR BY YOUR HOLY CROSS YOU HAVE REDEEMED
    THE WORLD.

READING   **MARK 15:29–31**

People passing by the cross shook their heads and
hurled insults at Jesus: "Aha! You were going to
tear down the Temple and build it back up in
three days! Now come down from the cross and
save yourself!" In the same way the chief priests
and teachers of the Law made fun of Jesus, saying
to one another, "He saved others, but he cannot
save himself! Let us see the Messiah, the king of
Israel, come down from the cross now, and we
will believe in him!"

(Pause for meditation.)

All who see me, jeer at me,
~Sneer at me, shaking their heads (Psalm 22:7).

Prayer
Lord Jesus Christ,
as you hung on the cross at noon,
mocked by priests, lawyers, and passersby,
the whole country was plunged into darkness
as the world mourned its Creator.
By the saving power of your cross,
grant us lasting light for our souls and bodies
and bring us in safety to the unfading glory
of our heavenly home,
where you live and reign forever and ever.
~Amen.

Seventh Station
Jesus between Two Criminals
We adore you, O Christ, and we bless you,
~For by your holy cross you have redeemed
the world.

Reading   **Luke 23:39–43**
One of the criminals hanging there hurled insults
at him: "Aren't you the Messiah? Save yourself
and us!" The other one, however, rebuked him,
saying, "Don't you fear God? You received the
same sentence he did. Ours, however, is only
right, because we are getting what we deserve for
what we did; but he has done no wrong." And he

said to Jesus, "Remember me, Jesus, when you come as King!" Jesus said to him, "I promise you that today you will be in Paradise with me."

(Pause for meditation.)

Christ suffered for sins once for all,
~THE RIGHTEOUS FOR THE UNRIGHTEOUS
(1 PETER 3:18).

PRAYER
Lord Jesus Christ,
as you were dying in agony at midafternoon,
you promised Paradise to a repentant criminal
before yielding up your spirit to your Father.
Innocent Jesus, who died to set us free,
soften our hard and stony hearts
and bring us to embrace in faith
the promise of Paradise made to all repentant
believers.
You live and reign there in glory, now and forever.
~AMEN.

Eighth Station
Jesus, Mary, and the Beloved Disciple
We adore you, O Christ, and we bless you,
~FOR BY YOUR HOLY CROSS YOU HAVE REDEEMED
THE WORLD.

READING   JOHN 19:25–27
Standing close to Jesus' cross were his mother, his

mother's sister, Mary the wife of Clopas, and
Mary Magdalene. Jesus saw his mother and the
disciple he loved standing there; so he said to his
mother, "He is your son!" Then he said to the disciple, "She is your mother." From that time the
disciple took her to live in his home.

(Pause for meditation.)

Look and see, all you who pass by,
~IF THERE IS ANY SORROW LIKE MY SORROW
(LAMENTATIONS 1:12).

PRAYER
Lord Jesus, giver of all good gifts,
even in your dying hour
you remembered the Woman
who heard and believed the Word of God.
May Mary, our Lady of Compassion,
be always our mother
and the mother of all who believe in you,
now and at the hour of our death.
~AMEN.

Ninth Station
The Dereliction and Death of Jesus
We adore you, O Christ, and we bless you,
~FOR BY YOUR HOLY CROSS YOU HAVE REDEEMED
THE WORLD.

At three o'clock Jesus cried out with a loud
shout, . . . "My God, my God, why did you abandon me?" Jesus knew that by now everything had
been completed; and in order to make the scripture come true, he said, "I am thirsty." A bowl was
there, full of cheap wine; so a sponge was soaked
in the wine, put on a stalk of hyssop, and lifted up
to his lips. Jesus drank the wine and said: "It is
finished!" Then he bowed his head and gave up
his spirit.

(Pause for meditation.)

I am poured out like water.
~YOU LAY ME IN THE DUST OF DEATH
   (PSALM 22:14, 15).

PRAYER
Lord Jesus Christ,
in your agony and bitter death,
you surrendered your spirit to your Father
and descended among the imprisoned spirits
to enlighten and release them.
Continue, in your mercy,
to break open the gates of death and hell
and to bring us at last to the resurrection of
   the body
and life everlasting in the world to come,
where you live and reign with the Father and the
   Holy Spirit,

one God, forever and ever.
~Amen.

Tenth Station
Testimony of the Roman Centurion

We adore you, O Christ, and we bless you,
~For by your holy cross you have redeemed
the world.

Reading   **Mark 15:37–41**

With a loud cry Jesus died. The curtain hanging in
the Temple was torn in two, from top to bottom.
The army officer who was standing there in front
of the cross saw how Jesus had died. "This man
was really the Son of God!" he said. Some women
were there, looking on from a distance. Among
them were Mary Magdalene, Mary the mother of
the younger James and of Joseph, and Salome.
They had followed Jesus while he was in Galilee
and had helped him. Many other women who had
come to Jerusalem with him were there also.

(Pause for meditation.)

All those sleeping in their graves
~Will wake up and sing for joy (Isaiah 26:19).

Prayer

Lord Jesus, Son of the living God,
when you bowed your head and gave up your
spirit,

the Roman centurion proclaimed you Son of God
as the watching women kept vigil for you.
Grant full pardon and fresh salvation
to those numbered among your faithful people
and raise up your servants who have fallen sleep
   in death,
O Savior of the world,
living and reigning, now and forever.
~AMEN.

Eleventh Station

Jesus' Side Is Pierced with a Lance

We adore you, O Christ, and we bless you,
~FOR BY YOUR HOLY CROSS YOU HAVE REDEEMED
   THE WORLD.

READING   **JOHN 19:31–34, 36–37**

Then the Jewish authorities asked Pilate to allow
them to break the legs of the men who had been
crucified, and to take the bodies down from the
crosses. So the soldiers went and broke the legs of
the first man and then of the other man who had
been crucified with Jesus. But when they came to
Jesus, they saw that he was already dead, so they
did not break his legs. One of the soldiers, however, plunged his spear into Jesus' side, and at
once blood and water poured out. This was done
to make the scripture come true: "Not one of
his bones will be broken." And there is another

scripture that says, "People will look at him whom they pierced."

(Pause for meditation.)

The Father sent his Son
~To be the Savior of the world (1 John 4:14).

PRAYER
Lord Jesus, living flame of love,
when you were pierced by the soldier's spear,
blood and water poured out at once,
a testimony to all who observed it.
May the sacred flood
that flowed from your broken heart
wash away all our sins,
sustain the living in faith,
grant eternal rest to the dead,
and bring us all to the house of life,
where we will praise, thank, and glorify
the Father, the Son, and the Holy Spirit,
forever and ever.
~Amen.

Twelfth Station
Blessed Are Those Who Mourn
We adore you, O Christ, and we bless you,
~For by your holy cross you have redeemed
the world.

When the people who had gathered there to watch the spectacle saw what happened, they all went back home, beating their breasts in sorrow. All those who knew Jesus personally, including the women who had followed him from Galilee, stood at a distance to watch.

(Pause for meditation.)

When we were baptized into union with Christ Jesus,

~WE WERE BAPTIZED INTO UNION WITH HIS DEATH (ROMANS 6:3).

PRAYER

With your martyred mother, Mary,
and the other women who had followed you from Galilee,
may we be filled, O Lord,
both with compassion for your sufferings
and with true sorrow for our sins.
As we look at your pierced and mangled body,
open the fountain of your mercy for us
through the gracious intercession of our Lady of Sorrows,
the chief mourner at your precious death and burial.

~AMEN.

Thirteenth Station

The Burial of Jesus

We adore you, O Christ, and we bless you,

~For by your holy cross you have redeemed
the world.

Reading   **Luke 23:50–54**

There was a man named Joseph from Arimathea,
a town in Judea. He was a good and honorable
man, who was waiting for the coming of the
Kingdom of God. Although he was a member of
the Council, he had not agreed with their deci-
sion and action. He went into the presence of
Pilate and asked for the body of Jesus. Then he
took the body down, wrapped it in a linen sheet,
and placed it in a tomb which had been dug out
of solid rock and which had never been used. It
was Friday, and the Sabbath was about to begin.

(Pause for meditation.)

I sleep secure at night,

~You keep me in your care (Psalm 4:8).

Prayer

Jesus, suffering servant of God,
on Good Friday evening
you rested in the sepulchre
and sanctified the grave
to be a bed of hope for your people:

Make us so repentant for our sins,
which were the cause of your passion,
that when our bodies lie in the dust,
our souls may live with you,
forever and ever.
~AMEN.

Fourteenth Station
Jesus' Body Rests in the Tomb
We adore you, O Christ, and we bless you,
~FOR BY YOUR HOLY CROSS YOU HAVE REDEEMED
   THE WORLD.

READING   **LUKE 23:55–56**
The women who had followed Jesus from Galilee
[Mary of Nazareth, Mary Magdalene, Mary the
mother of James and Joseph, Salome, and others]
went with Joseph and saw the tomb and how
Jesus' body was placed in it. Then they went back
home and prepared the spices and perfumes for
the body. On the Sabbath they rested, as the Law
commanded.

(Pause for meditation.)

Was it not necessary for the Messiah to suffer
   these things
~AND THEN TO ENTER HIS GLORY? (LUKE 24:26 TEV).

PRAYER

Lord Jesus Christ,
in your suffering you cried out to your Father,
and he delivered you out of death.
By the power of your life-giving cross,
rescue us from the abyss of sin
and flood our minds with the light of your
   resurrection,
O Savior of the world,
living and reigning with the Father and the Holy
   Spirit,
now and forever.
~Amen.

Prayer of Saint Bonaventure

O my God, good Jesus,
although I am in every way without merit and
   unworthy,
grant to me,
who did not merit to be present at these events
in the body,
that I may ponder them faithfully
in my mind
and experience toward you,
my God crucified and put to death for me,
that feeling of compassion
which your innocent Mother and the penitent
   Magdalene
experienced at the very hour of your passion.[99]

Notes

1. The Congregation for Divine Worship and the Discipline of the Sacraments, *Directory of Popular Piety and the Liturgy* (Vatican City, December 17, 2001), 5; see also 11.
2. *Directory* 7, 9, 15.
3. *Directory* 16.
4. Cf. *Directory* 19.
5. They are called "Grail Psalms" after the Ladies of the Grail, a lay apostolic group founded in the Netherlands but with an English offshoot that promoted this scholarly translation. The translation itself was done by a group of English Catholic Scripture scholars.
6. Evagrius of Pontus (c. 345–399), Sebastian Brock, *The Syriac Fathers* (Kalamazoo, Mich.: Cistercian Publications, 1987), 70–71
7. *Directory* 96–97.
8. First Sunday of Advent, Roman Sacramentary, International Committee on English in the Liturgy (hereafter cited as "ICEL").
9. Second Sunday of Advent, ICEL.
10. Third Sunday of Advent, ICEL.
11. Fourth Sunday of Advent, alternative prayer, ICEL.
12. Text based on Isaiah 40, ©St. Joseph Abbey, Spencer, MA, 1967, alt.
13. English Language Liturgical Consultation (hereafter cited as "ELLC").
14. ICEL collect, Dec. 20.
15. *Directory* 101–102.
16. *Nican Mopohua*, #22–23, trans. Virgil Elizondo, in *Guadalupe, Mother of the New Creation* (Maryknoll, N.Y.: Orbis Books, 1998), 7–8.
17. *Alma Redemptoris Mater,* trans. James Quinn, S.J., in *Praise for All Seasons* (Kingston, N.Y.: Selah, 1994), 97.
18. TEV.
19. ELLC.
20. *Book of Mary* (Washington, D.C.: BCL, 1987), 19.

21. ICEL, Dec. 12.
22. *Ave, Regina Caelorum,* trans. James Quinn, S.J., in *Praise for All Seasons,* 96.
23. ELLC.
24. This proclamation is from *The Old Roman Martyrology* and is often read out before Midnight Mass in monasteries and parishes alt.
25. ICEL, second Sunday after Christmas.
26. From the *Liber manualis minoritae* (Paris: Desclee, 1931), 98–101 alt.
27. *Directory* 114.
28. ELLC.
29. *The 1979 Book of Common Prayer* (New York: Oxford, 2003), 101.
30. *Directory* 114–115.
31. *Maria Aurora,* trans. Paul Cross, 1949, alt.
32. *Book of Mary,* 5.
33. ELLC.
34. *Directory* 117.
35. Cf. *Directory* 122.
36. Hymn text © 1974, Stanbrook Abbey, Callow End, Worcester WR2 4TD, UK.
37. TEV.
38. TEV.
39. Text is from *Praise God in Song,* John A. Melloh, S. M., and William G. Storey, eds. (Chicago: GIA Publications, 1979), 275.
40. ICEL, Epiphany, alternative prayer.
41. ICEL, February 2, opening prayer.
42. *Attende Domine,* from the Paris Processional of 1824, trans. Irvin Udulutsch, in *The Catholic Liturgy Book* (Baltimore: Helicon Press, 1975), #241.
43. Psalm 51 is attributed to King David (died c. 970 B.C.) after Nathan the prophet reproved him for adultery and murder. This is the classic psalm of repentance and the fourth of the penitential psalms.
44. TEV.
45. TEV.

46. Julian of Norwich, *Showings,* Edmund Colledge, O.S.A., and James Walsh, S.J., eds. (New York: Paulist Press, 1978), 200.

47. Trans. and adapted from "The XV oos in englysshe," in William Maskell, ed., *Monumenta Ritualia Ecclesiae Anglicanae,* vol. 2 (Oxford: Clarendon Press, 1846), 255–261.

48. TEV.

49. TEV.

50. TEV.

51. Text © 1974 and 1995, Stanbrook Abbey, Callow End, Worcester WR2 4TD.

52. *Directory* 138, 139.

53. From the Latin *Solus ad victimam procedis* by Peter Abelard (1079–1142), trans. Alan Gaunt, in *The Hymn Texts of Alan Gaunt* (London: Stainer and Bell 1991), 121–122.

54. See St. Bonaventure, O.F.M. (1217–1274), *Sermon 11 on Good Friday, Opera IX,* 265.

55. Sr. Mary Immaculate, C.S.C., ed., *The Tree and the Master* (New York: Random House, 1965), 48.

56. TEV.

57. TEV.

58. TEV.

59. *Directory* 141.

60. *Directory* 142.

61. © 1982 by The Church Hymnal Corporation, 800 Second Avenue, New York, NY 10017. Used by permission.

62. *Directory* 146.

63. *Directory* 147.

64. Trans. from the Middle English by Edmund Colledge, O.S.A., in *The Way* 19 (1979): 234–35.

65. Text: *Regina caeli laetare,* Latin, twelfth century.

66. Text: *Advenit veritas, umbra praeteriit,* Peter Abelard (1079–1142), trans. Alan Gaunt, in *Hymn Texts,* #110, 138–139.

67. ELLC.

68. Text: Latin, fifth century, trans. John Mason Neale (1851) and others.

69. Text: *Ad regias dapes,* 1632, trans. Robert Campbell (1814–1868), *St. Andrew's Hymnal,* 1850, alt.

70. Monks of New Skete, *Passion and Resurrection* (Cambridge, N.Y.: Monks of New Skete, 1995), Ode I, 227–28.

71. From a tenth-century Latin manuscript. Used with slight variations in William G. Storey, *A Seasonal Book of Hours* (Chicago: Liturgy Training Publications, 2002), 247–48.

72. Storey, *Seasonal,* 229.

73. Text: *Aurora lucis rutilat,* sixth century, trans. and adapted by Frank Quinn, O.P., et al.

74. *Directory* 156.

75. Text: *Veni, Creator Spiritus,* attributed to Rabanus Maurus (780–856), trans. John Webster Grant (1919-), in *Common Praise: Anglican Church of Canada* (Toronto: Anglican Book Centre, 1998), #638.

76. TEV.

77. Archbishop Stephen Langton (c. 1150/55–1228), *Veni, sancte Spiritus,* trans. John Webster Grant (1919–), *The Hymn Book of the Anglical Church of Canada and the United Church of Canada* (Toronto: [n.p.], 1994), #248.

78. Adapted by Charles Francis Whiston from an ancient prayer in Elizabeth Goudge, *A Diary of Prayer* (New York: Coward-McCann, 1966), 93.

79. *Directory* 158.

80. Text ©1974 Stanbrook Abbey, Callow End, Worcester WR2 4TD.

81. TEV.

82. ELLC.

83. ICEL, prayer for Trinity Sunday.

84. Text: St. Thomas Aquinas, O.P., *Adoro te devote,* trans. James Quinn, SJ, in *Praise for All Seasons,* 63.

85. Adapted from an ancient prayer of the Visigothic liturgy and from William Bright, *Ancient Collects* (Oxford: J.H. and James Parker, 1862), 142.

86. Julian of Norwich, *Showings,* 146.

87. Text: © 1974, Stanbrook Abbey, Callow End, Worcester WR2 4TD UK.

88. Many of the invocations of this litany can be traced to the seventeenth century. This litany was approved by Pope Leo XIII (1810–1903); see *A Book of Prayers* (ICEL, 1982), 24–25.

89. This litany was approved by Pope John XXIII (1881–1963) for the universal Church; see *Book of Prayers,* 26–27.

90. The invocations of this Litany of the Blessed Sacrament are drawn from several popular prayer books of the nineteenth and twentieth centuries.

91. A Marian litany containing some of these invocations was in use in the twelfth century. It was recorded in its present form (apart from a few additions by recent popes) at the shrine of Loreto in 1558 and was approved by Pope Sixtus V (1521–1590); see *Book of Prayers,* 28–29.

92. Approved by the Bishops' Committee on the Liturgy, National Conference of Catholic Bishops, USA, March 23, 1987; see *Book of Mary,* 27–29.

93. Louis Bouyer, *Introduction to Spirituality,* trans. Mary Perkins Ryan (Collegeville, Minn.: Liturgical Press, 1961), 87.

94. Text: Latin, eleventh century, trans. John Quinn, SJ, in *Prayers for All Seasons,* 97.

95. *Book of Prayers,* p. 35

96. *Book of Mary,* 7.94.

97. *Book of Prayers,* 34.

98. All the Scripture passages of the Way of the Cross are TEV.

99. Text: Trans. Ewert Cousins, in *Bonaventure* (New York: Paulist, 1978), 58.

Acknowledgments (cont.)

Excerpts from *Bonaventure: The Soul's Journey into God, The Tree of Life, The Life of St. Francis,* translation and introduction by Ewert Cousins; preface by Ignatius Brady, from The Classics of Western Spirituality, Copyright © 1978 by Paulist Press, Inc., New York/Mahwah, N.J. Used with permission of Paulist Press. www.paulistpress.com

Copyright material taken from *A New Zealand Prayer Book.* "He was despised and rejected," page 99, Copyright © 2002 is reprinted with permission of The General Secretary of New Zealand.

"A brightness glows o'er all the land" reprinted with permission of Frank C. Quinn, O.P. with extended rights to all future editions and to special nonprofit editions for use by the handicapped.

"God of fire and light," page 119, excerpted from *Lord Hear Our Prayer* ed. By Thomas McNally, C.S.C., and William Storey, D.M.S. Copyright © 2000 by Ave Maria Press, P.O. Box 428, Notre Dame, IN 46556, www.avemariapress.com. Used with permission of the publisher.

"Comfort my people" based on Isaiah 40, Copyright © Saint Joseph Abbey, Spencer, MA. Used with permission of the publisher.

"Holy, immortal, and living God," excerpted from *A Seasonal Book of Hours* by William G. Storey. Copyright © 2001 Archdiocese of Chicago: Liturgy Training Publications, 1800 North Hermitage Ave., Chicago, IL 60622. 1-800-933-1800. All rights reserved. Used with permission.

"*Nican Mopohua,*" #22–23, trans. Excerpted from *Guadalupe: Mother of the New Creation* by Virgil Elizondo. Copyright © 1998 Orbis Books, Maryknoll, NY. All rights reserved. Used with permission.

You Make Your Way Alone Words: Alan Gaunt © 1991 Stainer & Bell Ltd. Admin. By Hope Publishing Co., Carol Stream, IL 60188 All rights reserved. Used by permission.

Truly, He Comes to Us Words: Alan Gaunt © 1991 Stainer & Bell Ltd. Admin. By Hope Publishing Co., Carol Stream, IL 60188 All rights reserved. Used by permission.

"The love of God shown to all," "When Christ was born, God sent a star," "Mary crowned with living light," "Eternal Trinity of love," excerpted from *The Stanbrook Abbey Hymnal.* Copyright © 1974 Stanbrook Abbey.

The English translation of the Litanies of the Sacred Heart of Jesus, the Precious Blood of Jesus, and Our Lady (Loreto), and of the Ancient Prayer to the Virgin and the *Salve, Regina* from *A Book of Prayers* © 1982, International Committee on English in the Liturgy, Inc. (ICEL); the English Translation of the Opening Prayers from *The Roman Missal* © 1973, ICEL. All Rights Reserved.

English translation of the Te Deum Laudamus, the Benedictus, and the Magnificat prepared by the English Language Liturgical Consultation (ELLC), 1988.

Excerpts from the English translation of *The Roman Missal* © 1973, International Committee on English in the Liturgy, Inc. (ICEL); the English translation of the "Litany of the Blessed Virgin Mary" from the *Order of Crowning an Image of the Blessed Virgin Mary* © 1986, ICEL. All rights reserved.

"Ode I" of the Great Canon of Saint John of Damascus, excerpted from *A Book of Prayers,* by the monks of New Skete (Cambridge, NY, 1988), pp. 453–454.

Christmas Litany-PGIS © BY GIA PUBLICATIONS, INC. ALL RIGHTS RESERVED Psalms 2, 7, 8, 15, 16, 17, 22, 23, 33, 36, 47, 51, 54, 57, 62, 86, 93, 96, 117, 118, 145 © By Ladies Of The Grail (England). Used by permission of GIA Publications, Inc., exclusive agent. All rights reserved.

"The Five Sorrows of the Virgin," translated from the Middle English by Edmund Colledge, O.S.A., included in "Gracious Lady God's Mother," from *The Way,* 19 (1979), 234–235. Reprinted by kind permission of Way Publications, Oxford, U.K.

"O Queen of Heaven, to You the Angels Sing"
Text: *Ave, Regina Caelorum;* tr. James Quinn, S.J.
Text © James Quinn, S.J. Selah Publishing Co., Inc., North American agent.
www.selahpub.com

"Mother of Christ, Our Hope, Our Patroness"
Text: James Quinn, S.J.
Text © James Quinn, S.J. Selah Publishing Co., Inc., North American agent.
www.selahpub.com

"Jesus, Lord of Glory"
Text: St. Thomas Aquinas; para. James Quinn, S.J.
Text © James Quinn, S.J. Selah Publishing Co., Inc., North American agent.
www.selahpub.com

About the Editor

William G. Storey is professor emeritus of Liturgy and Church History at the University of Notre Dame. He has compiled, edited, and authored some of the best-loved prayer books of our time, most notably *Lord, Hear Our Prayer; Hail Mary: A Marian Book of Hours; An Everyday Book of Hours;* and *Mother of the Americas.* He currently resides in South Bend, Indiana.